¡Rise Up, Mi Gente!

A ROADMAP FOR LATINOS
TO ACHIEVE SUCCESS IN
CORPORATE AMERICA

. . .

Jesse A. Mejia

¡Rise Up, Mi Gente!
A Roadmap for Latinos to
Achieve Success in Corporate America
Jesse A. Mejia
Copyright © 2016 Jesse A. Mejia
All rights reserved.
Jesse@JesseMejiaSpeaks.com
http://JesseMejiaSpeaks.com
ISBN - 9780986118517
ISBN: 0986118516
Library of Congress Control Number: 2016914085
Catalyst Services Group, LLC, Bethesda, MD

For additional information, printable versions of the forms used in this book, and more tips and tools to promote a winning team culture, visit www.JesseMejiaSpeaks.com

No part of this publication may be reproduced, stored in a retrieval system, or transmitted in any form or by any means, electronic, mechanical, photocopying, recording, scanning, or otherwise, except as permitted under Section 107 or 108 of the 1976 United States Copyright Act, without the prior written permission of the Publisher. Requests to the Publisher for permission should be sent to Catalyst Services Group, LLC; Bethesda, Maryland.

¡Rise Up, Mi Gente!

LIMIT OF LIABILITY/DISCLAIMER OF WARRANTY:
The publisher and the author make no representations or warranties with respect to the accuracy or completeness of the contents of this work and specifically disclaim all warranties, including without limitation warranties of fitness for a particular purpose. No warranty may be created or extended by sales or promotional materials. The advice and strategies contained herein may not be suitable for every situation. This work is sold with the understanding that the publisher is not engaged in rendering legal, accounting, or other professional services. If professional assistance is required, the services of a competent professional should be sought. Neither the publisher nor the author shall be liable for damages arising herefrom. The fact that an organization or website is referred to in this work as a citation and/or a potential source of further information does not mean that the author or the publisher endorses the information that the organization or Web site may provide or any recommendations it may make. Further, readers should be aware that Internet Web sites listed in this work might have changed or disappeared between when this work was written and when it is read.

Printed in the United States

PROJECT MANAGER: John Peragine • john@johnpwriter.com

"The first category of people are always masters of the present, but the second are the lords of future."

- Fyodor Dostoevsky, Crime & Punishment

Contents

Acknowledgements · xiii
Introduction · xvii

Chapter 1   The Gift of a Poem · 1
                Soy Tu Hermano: My family's Story of Arrival in the
                U.S.A. · 6
                Evaluating Growth, Potential and Stereotypes · · · · · · · 11
                The Growth of the Latino Community · · · · · · · · · · · · 12
                Breaking the Mold · 20
                Become a Game Changer · 21
                Top 5 Challenges of First Generation MBA Applicants · · 23
Chapter 2   Passionate about Education · 27
                A New World · 33
                The Misconception with College Admissions · · · · · · · · 35
                Graduating from College with Options · · · · · · · · · · · · · 36
                Focus Factor 1: Personal Essays · · · · · · · · · · · · · · · · · · · 37
                Focus Factor 2: Work Experience · · · · · · · · · · · · · · · · · 40
                Focus Factor 3: The Interview · · · · · · · · · · · · · · · · · · · 42
                Focus Factor 4: Letters of Recommendation · · · · · · · · 46
                Focus Factor 5: Grade Point Average · · · · · · · · · · · · · · 49
                Focus Factor 6: Graduate Entrance Exams · · · · · · · · · · 51
                Martin's Story · 53
                The Four Types of MBA Programs: · · · · · · · · · · · · · · · · 57
                Rejected from Business School, Now What? · · · · · · · · · 60

Chapter 3	Balancing Heritage	63
	Master Networking on a Higher Level	64
	How to Network Within the Workplace	66
	You Pick, I Pay	68
	Preparing Your Elevator Pitch	69
	Real World Example #1:	70
	Real World Example #2	71
	Not all People are Created Equal	72
	From Pan Dulce to Bagels w/ Cream Cheese: The Art of Cultural Code Switching	72
	Valentina's Story	73
	How to Compete When You Don't Know How	78
	Marco's Story	78
	Recognizing the Social Cues of Interviewing	81
	The Art of Small Talk	83
	The Art of the Response	83
	Reading Body Language	84
	Don't Rock The Boat	85
Chapter 4	Latino History through Personal Stories	87
	Mario's Story	88
	Luis' Story	97
	Jocelyn's Story	99
	Daniela's Story	102
	Excy's Story	105
	Irene's Story	110
	Overcoming Hardship	113
Chapter 5	Being a Latino Leader in the 21st Century	114
	Tomas' Story	115
	Fitting in as a Latino	121
	To Have an MBA or Not	125
	Does Discrimination Really Occur?	125
	Javier's Story	127
	Selling Out	128

> Be Inclusive · 130
> Forge the Path for Latinos · · · · · · · · · · · · · · · · · · · 132
> The Growth of the Latino Leader · · · · · · · · · · · · · · · 132
> School Recognition · 133
> Accepting a Corporation Relocation Offer · · · · · · · · 133

Chapter 6 The Future of Latinos · 136

> About the Author · 139

Acknowledgements

• • •

I WANT TO THANK THE many people who gave me the inspiration, support, and confidence to write my perspective on a subject that I care about and have committed myself to improve.

My friends from the National Speakers Association who pushed me to write this book, and whose wisdom I followed. My coach, John Peragine, spent countless hours with me to draft this book from beginning to end. Without his technical ability, this book would not be what it is today. To my copy editor, K.C. Compton, thank you for editing my book and doing so with the finesse to keep my voice.

I want to thank the people I sought for their advice and contributions:

Dolores L. Arredondo
Gustavo Barbosa
Shaquita Basileo
Eloisa Martinez
James Padilla
Damali Rhett
Elvis Rodriguez
Dr. Deborah Santiago
Gil Valadez
Juan Vergara

Dedication

• • •

*Nothing would be possible without the support of my wife,
Liany Elba Arroyo.
Without her, this book will not get done.
Without her, my commitment to speak, coach or consult would not even be conceivable.
She is the reason for our family's success and I love her for that and for many other reasons that words alone cannot describe.
I am lucky I am married to a strong, Puerto Rican Woman.*

*While our daughter is only five years old and has no idea what I do for a living, it is her spirit and energy that serves as a daily reminder why it is important to have positive professional Latino role models in the lives of our young children.
They need to see that we too can wear business suits to work, dine at fine restaurants, attend elegant gala events, and serve on the boards of corporations and non-profit organizations to provide leadership.*

To our second child who will be born soon, I cannot finish this book without telling you that we already love you. We decided not to find out if you are a boy or a girl, because we want to cherish the surprise. Your presence will make us a stronger family and you will motive me further to continue to RISE UP!

Introduction

• • •

I AM THE SON OF Latino immigrants. I was born four months after my mother and father made their way to the United States, and I was raised in South-Central Los Angeles. My parents are from El Salvador, a nation that has been tarnished by devastating socioeconomic inequalities and decades of civil unrest, which eventually led to the country's 12-year civil war.

For most first generation Latinos, the beginning of my story is quite familiar. We are a community of people who feel pain, understand the emotional strain of living in poverty, but yet, somehow, we seem to find ways to rise up and stand tall with dignity. We are not yet known for being a community of financial wealth, but our work ethic, warmth and ability to endure has earned us a reputation of being a community of people filled with pride and perseverance.

My father was a landscaper and my mother, a housewife. Neither of my parents learned English well. In fact, they never had to learn English for two distinct reasons:

1. In Los Angeles, they lived their lives in a community that spoke Spanish.
2. They had me. At the age of seven, I was the official family translator. I would translate for my mother when she received letters from school, when the doctor gave us our check-ups, and I even translated for my father when he had to negotiate prices when he bid on landscaping jobs, such as tree removal, lawn mowing and trimming, or grounds maintenance.

Jesse A. Mejia

For most, it is no surprise that *we as Latinos* have to learn how to master life in a bilingual and bicultural world from a young age. I attribute this skill to our instinctive ability to adapt and endure. We are an American community that continuously has had to withstand indignities from employers, politicians, pundits, and, sadly, fellow Americans.

However, we are a new generation of Latinos. We have been raised in the U.S.A., educated here, and are eager to set a stronger foothold in America. While our parents might have served in the roles of laborers in a blue-collar America, today, we are determined to enhance our legacy as we pursue our careers in Corporate America. Struggle is not new to us. The word "no" is not new to us and like our parents, and our parents' parents, we will find our way too. Breaking into a well-paying job in Corporate America is not easy, especially when our parents are not in a position to provide us advice on how to do so. Navigating through the channels of corporate politics, learning how to network, and realizing that hard work will not always get you ahead may be new challenges for you, but in time you will learn how to overcome these hurdles too.

The purpose of this book is to share my opinion, provide examples of how other Latinos achieved success and offer my story on how I was able to find success in Corporate America. I will walk you through the life lessons I have learned and the lessons I share with other Latinos as I help them navigate their path to enriching careers in highly competitive industries such as investment banking, consulting, marketing, and more.

I chose to refer to this book as a roadmap to illustrate how other Latinos found success, while taking the approaches that were the best for them. While your path may take some twists and turns, stay the course, because NOTHING is a straight shot to success in Corporate America. There is no one path to achieve success. I will show you the challenges others had to overcome, and share with you their story on how they achieved their goals. I am passionate about Latino success because I simply care about our community. I care about people, and I want my people to achieve greatness. I love that we are humble, hardworking families, and our time to become more ambitious has arrived. Many paths exist that can lead you to your individual goals, but until someone shows you a way, we as a community will never be able to pursue any.

¡Rise Up, Mi Gente! I ask you to read this book so you can be better prepared to achieve more. Invest in your professional development so you can become more competitive when you pursue high-paying jobs, and most importantly, encourage others to *Rise Up* as well because our community needs a strong generation of high-income earners so we can emotionally and financially support the rising generation that will follow us.

CHAPTER 1

The Gift of a Poem

• • •

IT WAS APRIL 18, 2015, and I was at New Rochelle High School in New Rochelle, New York. The school was hosting its 2nd annual Latino Youth Leadership Conference and I was the invited keynote speaker. Mr. Gustavo Barbosa, one of the school's four house principals, had sought me out a couple months earlier and invited me to speak at the event. Gustavo was born in Colombia, but came to the U.S.A. at a young age. His personal story on how he had succeeded in America, as a Latino immigrant, moved me. He stressed to me how this leadership conference was student-run, student-funded, and student-focused. Gustavo passionately described the day as, "a day of celebration, unity, inspiration, development and Latino empowerment." He explained to me how this event would be a forum for teens to build their skills, celebrate their strengths, hear from successful Latino role models, and become inspired to follow their dreams and pursue a future filled with opportunities. With such a powerful and motivating effort, I was eager to be part of the event.

What had a greater impact on me was when Gustavo also asked me to lead a workshop for the parents to discuss how, as Latino immigrants, they could best help support their children to achieve success in school and in their lives. Most of the parents had to make special arrangements and take great measures in order to be in attendance. I was excited to facilitate the discussion and the parents were eager to ask me questions on how I developed my career so they too could encourage their children to follow in similar footsteps. I was proud to be the keynote speaker, not solely because I could share my experience with the students, but because I was also able to help the parents answer many of their questions about how to pick a college major and how to determine a career after graduation. I provided financial literacy tips regarding student loans, gave my opinion on when to start looking for a summer internship, and my personal favorite, discussed how to approach the graduate school application process. These parents were like my parents, loving and supportive, but unfamiliar on how to navigate life after high school – much less life after college. My parents had struggled mightily about how to guide me in college and with the early stages of my career, so I was keenly aware of the struggles these parents were having, and helping them was a gratifying experience for me. However, little did I know that my most gratifying experience would be listening to a young lady in her junior year at the high school, recite a poem about the strength of Latinos, written by the man who invited me to speak, Mr. Gustavo Barbosa.

Gustavo Barbosa had decided to write his own poem to express his love for our Latino culture and to highlight the warmth, commitment and pride of our people. While I went to the conference expecting to be one of the main contributors on the topic of Latino Leadership, I actually walked away with a deeper sense of pride in what it means to be a Latino. Leadership is about helping others grow. While sometimes we may not always want to help each other, we should recognize that we do depend on one another to progress. Latinos come in many shades of brown, with our heritage rooted in Europe, Africa, the Caribbean, Central, South or North America, and we will always find ourselves in situations where we have to explain who we are to others. This is a reality that will not escape us. Embrace your culture, be proud of your experience, and share out loud your ambition to be great!

I am proud to share this poem with you.

¿Preguntas Quién Soy? – Are You Wondering Who I am?
By: Gustavo Barbosa

Soy la riqueza de Costa Rica
And the strength of the Andes.
Soy bella como Quisquella,
Y luchador como Ecuador.
Soy Caribe, Pacifico, y Atlántico
Panama connects me y El Caribe me inspira.
I can touch the sky in Machu Picchu.
I am the center of the world in the Galapagos.

I am Inca, Maya, Garífuna, Azteca, y Taina.
Soy descendiente de grandes civilizaciones,
Pirámides, brain surgery, and the concept of zero.
Soy Moctezuma, la Malinche, Atahualpa, y Túpac Amaru.
Yo no coloreé mi continente, ni dividí mi gente.
Soy lo que dejaron, soy el oro que se robaron.
"El descubrimiento," me duele recordarlo y no puedo celebrarlo.
After 500 years, there is nothing to celebrate.

The blood of Africa corre por mis venas
Y sus tambores alegran mi corazón.
I am the Quilombos and the Palenques
Soy la libertad de Benkos Biohó
I am dark and sweet como la Melaza
More than 150 million Afro-descendientes
Making our continent better and stronger.
A history stolen, but not forgotten.

Soy América latina, soy la Pachamama
Un pueblo sin piernas pero que camina.
Same dreams, desires, and suffering

Jesse A. Mejia

I am Bolivar's dream of "La Gran Colombia."
El Panamericanismo me inspira
And the Unity of our people motivates me.
I can fight for Independence like José
Martí, Hidalgo, y San Martin,
Or unite my community like César Chávez.

My hips move to merengue, punta, bachata y salsa
I dance to the tambores of Cuba.
El acordeón de Colombia me enamora
Soy la marimba de Honduras y el mariachi de México.
Soy vallenatos, corridos, y perico ripiao;
Soy cumbia, banda, y regetton.
Sometimes I cry listening
To rancheras, tangos o boleros de los abuelos.

We are the people of corn:
Tortillas, arepas y pupusas.
Maíz defines me, maíz is who I am
Corn is who you are!
I am beans, frijoles, or habichuelas.
No matter what you call them,
Habichuelas taste better,
When cooked by las abuelas.

Soy Mestizo, soy blanco, soy negra, soy mulata.
Hermana, comadre, paisano, parcero, mi pana!
Mi cuate, compadre, mi socio, Mi hermano – mi brother,
Somos todos vecinos, y todos hermanos
They call me boricua,
Me dicen catracho, guanaco, chapin, pibe.
Me dicen cholita, ñaña, chama, paisana
Todas hijas de Dios, todas hermanas, todas hispanas.

I believe …
I believe in Santa Rosa de Lima, and the Orishas of Cuba.
Soy la virgen de Guadalupe y el indio Juan Diego
Soy el Divino Niño y el Cristo Negro.
I celebrate and honor those who came before me
I am "El Día de Los Muertos."
Soy todos los Santos que cuelgan de mi cuello
Soy un escapulario y mil rosarios.

I did not cross the border, the border crossed me!
I am the Gonzalez, Hernandez, or Garcia,
Who lived in Tejas, Arizona, California, or Puerto Rico
Before that land was taken by the U.S.A.
I am the Garcia, Hernandez, or Gonzalez
Who crossed the Rio Grande yesterday
And with my daily labor, sudor y ganas
Will improve the America of tomorrow.

Illegal immigration started in 1492,
I have the same dreams as the Pilgrims.
Soy balsero, soy mojado, soy indocumentado, soy humano.
I am not an alien, I am a human being.
Trabajo duro, and I do not take jobs away from anyone.
I build, I farm, I clean, I teach, I inspire, I protect.
I can be the professional of the Silicon Valley,
Or the campesino of the Hudson Valley.

I am the child of immigrants.
I am an "unaccompanied" minor.
With hard work, dedication and education
Voy de menor a mayor, como Sonia Sotomayor.
I am on the Bodegas of Main Street,
And the offices of Wall Street.

A day without a Mexican?
Be careful what you wish for!

Yo soy David, Jesús, María, Daniel, o Raquel,
I Am Rachel, Daniel, Maria, Jesus, or David.
Hablo español, quechua, mam, guarani, o chichimeca.
I communicate as easily in English or Spanglish.
I dream in two languages
Yo amo en dos idiomas.
At seven years old, I can be the official family translator;
When mami needs to talk to doctors, landlords, or teachers.

¿Todavía Preguntas Quién Soy? – Are You
Still Wondering Who I am?

This is who I am:

Soy latina, soy hispana, soy tu hermana.
Soy latino, soy hispano, soy tu hermano

By Gustavo Barbosa

Soy Tu Hermano: My family's Story of Arrival in the U.S.A.

As your hermano, I want to share with you my family's story. It is important to me that you understand that my beginning is similar to your beginning. My parents' financial troubles may parallel those your family has had or is experiencing. My advice is rooted in a trench of strength, struggle, sacrifice, brotherhood, equality, leadership, and love. I do not give advice based on theory, but rather on a proven path where I have helped others also achieve their goals. My story is the Latino American story and

I stress this because I believe that it is important for people to know where they came from and to understand their personal history. This becomes especially paramount for families who have made the sacrifices to travel to the U.S.A. I also want to share my family's story so you can understand what we endured in order to find success in America.

I was born in Los Angeles, but my parents are originally from El Salvador. Being an underdeveloped country, there was already a struggle to survive. Coffee was the primary crop in the country, responsible for nearly all of the income in the country. However, the wealth was restricted to only the top few of the population, creating a stark imbalance in financial stability. Job opportunities were incredibly limited, and there was no opportunity for upward mobility. Most people in El Salvador were focused on basic survival.

On top of the economic struggles, El Salvador was rife with political turmoil, as its civil war was imminent and inevitable. The income disparity between its citizens fostered an environment of tension and unhappiness as people couldn't meet their basic needs. My parents could see what was going on around them, and while they wanted to raise a family, they did not want to do it in a country that was about to become war-torn.

My mother was pregnant with me and they were facing a reality that their home country would never be a stable place to raise a family. They were like any parent – they wanted to ensure a better life for their child than the one that they had. My father decided that he was going to sell what he could, so that he and my mother could start a life in the United States. At the time, my father owned an old, rundown Volkswagen Beetle, which he sold to make sure he had the money necessary for passage and to make strides for a brighter future.

My parents made their way to Tijuana, Mexico and were ready to cross the border. They were on their own, with nothing to guide them than the desire to get to the United States. My father's plan was to help my mother cross first, as they had a family friend waiting for them in Los Angeles to pick up my mother. While the plan was partially firm, the biggest challenge was how to cross the border and get to L.A. My father noticed that an American tour group was shopping in Tijuana, and saw that their Greyhound bus was parked waiting for their group to board. On the front of the bus, their destination plate read Los Angeles and my dad quickly realized that was my mother's best chance to get to L.A. to meet up with their friend. My father encouraged my mother to take the risk and hop on the bus. Fortunately my mother had brown hair, was fair skinned and had green eyes. To most people, she did not look like she was from El Salvador. So as she built up her courage to begin her journey, she prayed. Her nerves were high, she was scared of being caught, but she looked as though she belonged. From afar, my father witnessed my mother walk across the border and board the bus. He too was praying that she would not get caught, and as more passengers boarded the bus, the more he feared that she would be outed. Within 20 minutes of my mother boarding, the Greyhound bus left Tijuana and began its drive to Los Angeles. Just like that, my mother was now in America. No one questioned her.

My father had a different story. My father looked like he was from El Salvador. His Mayan indigenous features were strong—his dark olive skin, straight black hair and thin, square body frame would have given him away if he tried the same approach as my mother. Instead, my father stood still as he watched my mother seamlessly cross over to San Diego as she headed to Los Angeles. While relieved, my father was now alone and my mother, pregnant with me, suddenly found herself alone in a completely new country. My parents had not been apart from each other since their wedding day and now, they were worlds away. My father's level of urgency to find a way back to my mother rose exponentially and he explored the limited options available to him.

Tijuana has an underground economy of men and women who help others cross the border. My father found a coyote to guide his passage across the desert. Coyotes basically smuggle people across the border for a fee. Coyotes themselves are often dangerous, mostly because they view their clients as cargo and not so much as human life. Even if the coyotes are compassionate, the trip itself is treacherous. My father found himself with a small group of other folks who were also making their way to America. My dad was thin, so he and three others were crammed into the trunk of a Chevy headed to Los Angeles. With others who were also desperate to escape their circumstances back home and make a new life in America, they made the drive successfully to Los Angeles.

My parents were dedicated to giving me a better future. My father had been adamant that he did not want his son to be born into a country full of violence and poverty. There had to be something better out there for him – for his family. They sacrificed everything they had and risked their own lives to come to America so that I had a chance to succeed.

What most non-immigrants choose not to recognize is that simply arriving in the United States does not guarantee success. My parent's journey didn't guarantee their success or mine: It only gave them a chance to seek employment in a country that had opportunity for those willing to work low wage jobs. While America was nothing like El Salvador, it did share that country's sense of struggle. The Latino immigrant still has to struggle and sacrifice in order to progress, and that's what my parents dedicated themselves to doing.

Initially, my father had many odd jobs but later settled as a landscaper. For some reason, landscaping is the work that many Latinos immigrants find themselves doing, and in our case, my father did well at it. Even though his income was low, he always found clients, while never learning how to properly speak English. My father was always motivated by the need to make sure his family was taken care of and that we at least had a chance to do something productive. My mother stayed home with my little sister and me. My father gradually built his business into owning his own truck and landscaping route, meaning he had several houses he maintained and he would landscape between three to five homes, six days a week over a two-week rotation. My father charged low, so he had to work multiple homes in order to make a tiny profit. My father hit "pay dirt" when he landed a seven-acre property that required full-time attention. The man who owned the land paid my father $1,200 a month to take care of the property. That became our family's budget, but it was consistent and minimized his gasoline expense. My father worked that property for 14 years and we all experienced financial stability during that time.

To us, my father was successful, but to American standards we were part of the lower class. There were many other Americans who had more money and status, and therefore, more opportunity. As a child I was acutely aware of differences in class and status. The differences are obvious by the stereotyped Latinos portrayed on television.

Having parents who struggled with English meant they just were not capable of interacting with my teachers, neighbors or other parents without my help to translate. This created isolation for my family. We spoke with accents. We looked Latino, but it was not until much later that I realized this life experience fostered an extremely valuable skill: versatility.

I learned from a young age how to digest information and repeat it to my parents in a manner that they could understand. This not only forced me to be a great listener, it also forced to me hone my comprehension skills. I knew how to read non-verbal social cues, which served me well in my adult career. To be a leader, I had to learn how to live in a world of gray. I was poor, others were not, my parents did not speak English, and others did not speak Spanish. I was the cultural bridge and the liaison to the American society.

I am sure that you too have had to wear many hats for your family, and that ability to interact in various worlds makes you valuable. What you need to do now is learn how to sell it! I will show you how I did it, and my hope is that you will learn from my experience.

Evaluating Growth, Potential and Stereotypes

In describing the richness of Latino culture, taking pride in our civic contributions and hearing how much we as Latinos matter to businesses and in political elections, there is also a story of stereotypes that we must recognize. In America, Latinos are the subject of news reports, political stump speeches, comedy sketches and the focus of jokes – none of which is flattering. Even when we hear and see these stereotypes, what do many of us do?

We remain silent.

We smile.

We nod.

But what is going on inside us? We often hate those speaking, hate how out of place we feel, and we may even feel some shame ourselves. As Latinos, we may seek the path of least resistance, and so not only do we enable the misconceptions to continue, we become the stereotype.

There were times when I felt out of place, not sure what my next move should be, but I grew the courage to dream big. Now, I have earned my MBA and I am a businessman. I decided to not remain silent, and I did not accept the career path of a stereotypical Latino landscaper. My father was a proud man and a hard worker, and, though I was the son of a landscaper, he too wanted more for me, even though he did not know how to help me. Nonetheless, I found ways to help myself, and I surrounded myself with those who believed in me and had the knowledge to help me achieve my professional goals – to become a successful Latino businessman and leader.

Whether you are a young professional, an established professional or even a parent, as I am now, and you want you or your children to achieve big things, I can tell you there is a path to achieve those goals.

In our American society, corporate culture plays a role in the pursuit of your ambitions. While every corporation claims to be an Equal Opportunity Employer, there will always be favorites. There will always be a "good ole' boys club" you will not be invited to join. There will always be someone who does not merit the opportunity to be on the "fast track," yet there they are. There will always be someone who is getting ahead, and it will have nothing to do with intellectual capability, but everything to do with the corporate culture that you have submersed yourself into. Culture and corporations do not change easily, and regardless of your personal feelings, it is your job to rise above. It is your job to accept that the company rational for promoting someone else will be because they were "just a better fit for the role," whereas in reality, it could have been as simple as the hiring manager not wanting to introduce a dynamic that he or she was not familiar with and running the risk of disrupting the team dynamics. In an effort to overcome these barriers, it is also your job to be well prepared. Meet your challenges with presence, polish and poise. Invest in your professional development so it will be hard for anyone to deny your success.

I am passionate about this topic because I too continue to face these same challenges every day, but I meet each challenge with confidence. Learning how to overcome adversity is a skill that is learned over time, and this, *mi gente*, is what is called: GRIT. In Spanish, we call Grit – GANAS, and it will be the GANAS that you possess that will set you apart as you push through the challenges that you will face. As Latinos, we come from a powerful and proud heritage of people who know how to excel in the face of adversity. Grit is in our blood! Stay focused, stay positive, stay professional, and move forward.

The Growth of the Latino Community

As Latinos, our numbers are growing. In 2000, there were 35.2 million Latinos in the United States. The Pew Research Center reports that in 2014, 55.3 million Latinos live in the U.S.A., comprising 17.3% of the total U.S. population. This is a 57% increase in 14 years. Per the Pew Hispanic Research Center, our numbers will soar to 119 million by 2060.

Table 1 STATISTICAL PORTRAIT OF HISPANICS IN THE UNITED STATES, 2014 **Population, by Race and Ethnicity: 2014**		
Universe: 2014 resident population		
	Population	Percent
Hispanic	55,250,517	17.3
U.S. born	35,949,570	11.3
Foreign born	19,300,947	6.1
White alone, not Hispanic	197,441,410	61.9
Black alone, not Hispanic	39,302,196	12.3
Asian alone, not Hispanic	16,501,080	5.2
Other, not Hispanic	10,361,853	3.2
Total	**318,857,056**	**100.0**

Note: "Other, not Hispanic" includes persons reporting single races not listed separately and persons reporting more than one race.

Source: Pew Research Center tabulations of 2014 American Community Survey (1% IPUMS)

PewResearchCenter

The Pew Research Center compared numbers from the 2000 and 2010 census and reported that Latinos also account for 17.3% of all Americans. This means we are also 17.3% of the buying power in America. If Latinos were a country, our sheer size would make us the 24th largest country on the planet. More importantly, a 2015 study completed by the Selig Center for Economic Growth at the University of Georgia's Terry College of Business, states that the U.S. Latino buying power is $1.3 trillion. That figure exceeds the buying power of all but 13 countries in the world. This statistic is critical because it means that Latinos in America buy as many goods as countries such as Canada, Russia and Australia, yet our clout in the United States has yet to been fully realized.

During the time frame from 1980 to 2000 there was a huge growth of Latinos in America due to immigration, from 4.2 million to over 14 million.

Our numbers are growing, but our reputation to achieve iconic CEO status or high profile leadership roles within Corporate America has not.

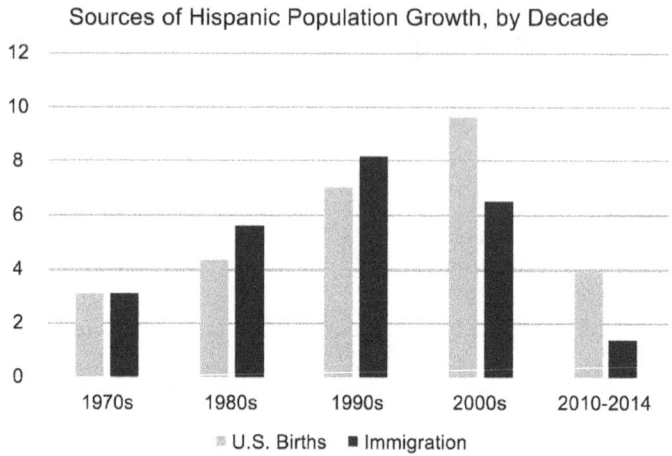

Source: Note: U.S. births and immigrations reflect additions to the U.S. Hispanic population. Deaths and emigration not shown.
Source: Based on Pew Research Center tabulations of 2014 American Community Survey (1% IPUMS) for 2010-2014, and of the 2010 American Community Survey (1% IPUMS) for 2000s. Data for 1970s, 1980s and 1990s drawn from Pew Research Center historical projections (Passel and Cohn, 2008).
Pew Research Center

Per the chart above, you can see that we could be able to leverage our strength in numbers. More importantly, are you beginning to wonder why we are not better represented in areas, such as business or politics? According to the Hispanic Association on Corporate Responsibility (HACR), Latinos continue to be underrepresented at the highest levels in Corporate America, but the HACR highlights that in 2015, there were 10 Latino CEOs of Fortune 500 companies. We have potential for that number to be larger and, with our population, it is not unreasonable to believe that we can be represented at the 17.3 % mark or more within our professional discipline.

So, when I say, "¡Rise Up, Mi Gente!," I intend it as a call to action to take a more prominent role within our society, because our numbers are increasing. We must shed any outdated stereotypes of what a Latino is perceived to be and refocus our energy on what our community needs. As Latinos, we need to have a solid footing in our careers so we can become national leaders and help influence change. Let the new stereotype be that Latinos are polished, intelligent, and heavily sought-after as business men and women, innovators, and leaders in all areas of life. You or your parents made it here with that dream – now it is time to make that next step, to secure your future and your legacy.

To my hermanos and hermanas who identify as millennials, I want to share some statistics especially targeted to you. According to the Pew Research Center analysis of the U.S. Census Bureau data, Latinos are the youngest major racial group in the United States. Approximately 14.6 million Latinos are millennials and youth is a defining characteristic for the overall Latino population in America. Specifically, out of the eligible voters who are Latino, 44% are Latino millennials. More impressive, Latinos represent 21% of all U.S. millennials. In contrast, we Latinos only make up 15% of the total U.S. adult population. Latino millennials will be the heartbeat of our community and country, and our millennials will serve a pivotal importance as how we will change the face of our nation.

The Generations Defined

The Millennial Generation	Generation X	The Baby Boom Generation
Born: 1981 to 1996*	Born: 1965 to 1980	Born: 1946 to 1964
Age of adults in 2014: 18 to 33	Age in 2014: 34 to 49	Age in 2014: 50 to 68

The Silent Generation	The Greatest Generation	
Born 1928 to 1945	Born: Before 1928	
Age in 2014: 69 to 86	Age in 2014:87 and older	

* The youngest Millennials are in theirteens. No chronological endpoint has been set for this group.

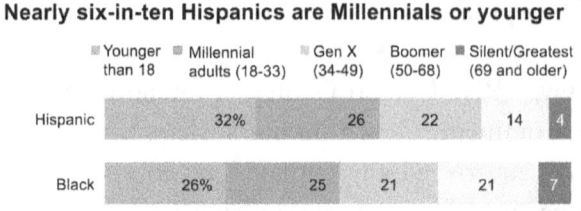

The Hispanic population is the nation's youngest major racial or ethnic group.
Source: *Pew Hispanic Center tabulations of 2011 American Community Survey (1% IPUMS)*

The Hispanic population is the nation's **youngest** *major racial or ethnic group*

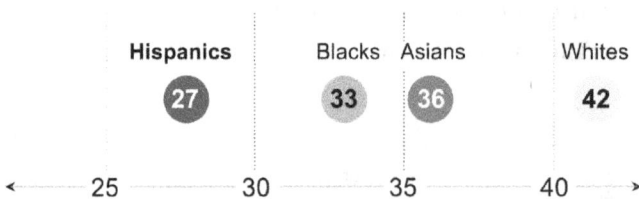

Pew Research Hispanic Center tabulations of 2011 American Community Surver (1% IPUMS)

Now, as our parents have told us, our potential lies in our level of education.

The hope lies in that the number of hispanic adults with a high school diplomas has increased from 52% to 63% between 2000 and 2011.

A greater share of Hispanic adults have **high school diplomas** *today than in 2000.*

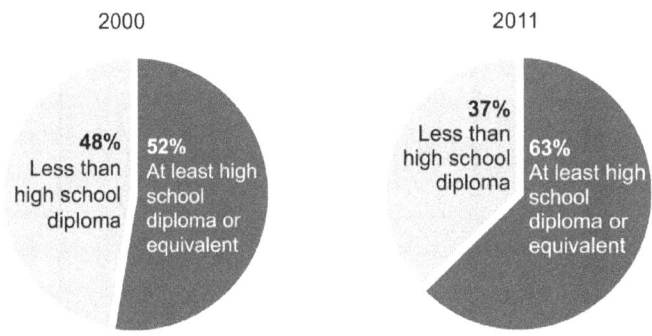

Pew Research Hispanic Center tabulations of 2011 American Community Survey (1% IPUMS)

When I was growing up, my mother had a saying that I believe many Latino households are extremely familiar with:

• • •

Dime con quien ANDAS, y te dire quien eres.
– translation-
Tell who you are with and I will tell you who you are !

• • •

Table 17
STATISTICAL PORTRAIT OF HISPANICS IN THE UNITED STATES, 2014
Educational Attainment, by Race and Ethnicity: 2014

Universe: 2014 resident population ages 25 and older

	Less than 9th grade	9th to 12th grade	High school graduate	Two-year degree/Some college	Bachelor's degree or more	Total
Hispanic	6,333,358	4,280,729	8,317,490	7,333,545	4,432,492	30,697,614
U.S. born	1,007,263	1,634,314	4,062,154	4,685,147	2,637,856	14,026,734
Foreign born	5,326,095	2,646,415	4,255,336	2,648,398	1,794,636	16,670,880
White alone, not Hispanic	3,475,086	7,847,854	39,996,898	42,968,965	47,756,710	142,045,513
Black alone, not Hispanic	1,050,579	2,760,468	7,800,435	8,158,524	4,867,343	24,637,349
Asian alone, not Hispanic	942,434	626,482	1,760,281	2,228,508	5,953,222	11,510,927
Other, not Hispanic	208,163	408,374	1,320,162	1,684,184	1,293,513	4,914,396
Total	**12,009,620**	**15,923,907**	**59,195,266**	**62,373,726**	**64,303,280**	**213,805,799**
PERCENT DISTRIBUTION						
Hispanic	20.6	13.9	27.1	23.9	14.4	100.0
U.S. born	7.2	11.7	29.0	33.4	18.8	100.0
Foreign born	31.9	15.9	25.5	15.9	10.8	100.0
White alone, not Hispanic	2.4	5.5	28.2	30.3	33.6	100.0
Black alone, not Hispanic	4.3	11.2	31.7	33.1	19.8	100.0
Asian alone, not Hispanic	8.2	5.4	15.3	19.4	51.7	100.0
Other, not Hispanic	4.2	8.3	26.9	34.3	26.3	100.0
All	**5.6**	**7.4**	**27.7**	**29.2**	**30.1**	**100.0**

Note: "High school graduate" includes persons who have attained a high school diploma or its equivalent, such as a General Educational Development (GED) certificate. "Other, not Hispanic" includes persons reporting single races not listed separately and persons reporting more than one race.

Source: Pew Research Center tabulations of 2014 American Community Survey (1% IPUMS)

PewResearchCenter

Table 17
STATISTICAL PORTRAIT OF HISPANICS IN THE UNITED STATES, 2014
College Enrollment, by Race and Ethnicity: 2014

Universe: 2014 resident population ages 18 through 24

	ENROLLED IN COLLEGE	ENROLLMENT RATE
Hispanic	2,363,761	35.4
U.S. born	1,970,697	38.3
Foreign born	393,064	25.7
White alone, not Hispanic	7,703,008	44.4
Black alone, not Hispanic	1,650,132	35.6
Asian alone, not Hispanic	1,067,662	65.3
Other, not Hispanic	514,706	40.4
Total	**13,299,269**	**42.1**

Universe: 2014 resident population ages 25 and older

	ENROLLED IN COLLEGE	ENROLLMENT RATE
Hispanic	1,383,862	4.5
U.S. born	923,205	6.6
Foreign born	460,657	2.8
White alone, not Hispanic	5,415,802	3.8
Black alone, not Hispanic	1,695,677	6.9
Asian alone, not Hispanic	783,769	6.8
Other, not Hispanic	345,639	7.0
Total	**9,624,749**	**4.5**

Note: "Other, not Hispanic" includes persons reporting single races not listed separately and persons reporting more than one race.

Source: Pew Research Center tabulations of 2014 American Community Survey (1% IPUMS)

PewResearchCenter

My father stopped attending school after the third grade. My mother stopped attending school after the ninth grade. Both my parents instilled in me the certainty that school was critical to my success. I am confident your parents instilled the same value in you. Sometimes, not everyone in our families wants to listen. Whether you are a millienial, the parent of a millennial or a professional who is thinking about going back to school to earn an advanced degree, take a moment to digest the next table that highlights the levels of education attained by our Latino community.

In 2014, there were approximately 30.7 million Latinos over the age of 25. When compared to the other ethiniticies, the Latino community has the lowest percentage of individuals who have completed a bachelor's degree. The majority of our population only has a high school diploma, followed by those who only completed an associate's degree or have some college but never finished.

The story does shift for Latino millennials, focused between the ages of 18 through 24, there are 2.4 million enrolled in college, representing a 35.4% enrollment rate. Though still lagging behind other enthnicities in America, we are making progress, and the sacrifices that our parents have made to ensure a better life for their children is beginning to pay off with the millenial generation. Nevertheless, with the numbers of Latinos growing in America, there should be even greater numbers of high school graduates and even more importantly, the numbers of undergrads and graduate students should also increase.

Let's work together to make this happen. Let me show you how!

Breaking the Mold

To be a leader, especially as a Latino, you need to understand how to navigate the cultural systems in Corporate America, which requires a balancing act of heritage, community, family, and personal drive. Often, people to help you are few and far between, blocked by context or language barriers.

The key to understanding leadership, and how Latinos can become leaders, is to know the pieces of the puzzle. Identifying the challenges that Latinos in America face helps create conversation and works to build paths that can change the status quo. It is imperative to me that I work to show that it is possible to get a great education and have a great career.

It would have been easy for me to fall in line behind my father and become an entirely honorable landscaper. Children tend to follow in their parents' footsteps and do as they do because it is what the young people know. I want to change their scenery so that they can see the bigger picture and use their challenges as footholds to keep climbing.

Become a Game Changer

In 2007, I started helping ambitious individuals apply to business school so they too could earn their Master of Business Administration. Initially, I was helping my circle of friends, who were mostly Latino. Overtime, non-Latinos began to reach out to me because they were confronting the same challenges we had because they too were first generation college graduates. I quickly realized that if there is no one in your life to help create a roadmap for you to follow, then you are on a path to nowhere. A roadmap is exactly what we need! No one has all the answers, I do not have all the answers, but I know where to go when questions arise. This, my friends, is the essence of my book: knowing where to go when you want to make your life better.

Since I believe in pursuing careers in Corporate America, a quick way to get on the fast track is to pursue an MBA. I am passionate about Latinos having an MBA because in my experience I have seen it as a game-changing degree. As someone who was deathly afraid of math in high school, I chose a college major that did not require any math – Speech Communication. In college, I was thrilled because I was studying a topic that I enjoyed and did not have to relive the bad experience I had in high school.

Soon after I graduated from college it became obvious that I needed to understand accounting, financial statement analysis and finance if I wanted a career in business. I invested in myself and began taking Calculus, Statistics, and Accounting classes at a local college after work so I could revamp my math skills. Not only did I come to terms that the subject is not that tough with the right teacher, I also got the bug to go back to school and earn my Master of Business Administration.

I always wanted to be a corporate executive, but I did not always know how until I observed that many of the white men who were executives for the company I worked for had their MBAs. So I wanted to be like them. As I researched schools, I recognized that not all MBA programs were equal. While some folks can find success by pursuing an MBA degree online or part-time, today, I coach the men and women I help to pursue their MBA on a fulltime basis from a Top 25 program.

An MBA is that one flexible graduate degree that will give you instant credibility to pursue whatever endeavor you want, even if you have not figured out yet what you want to do. An MBA can catapult your salary and even position you financially to be able to support your parents, who may depend on you for their wellbeing. For all the wonderful and encouraging benefits an MBA can provide, applying to business school is undeniably a humbling, overwhelming, and emotionally draining personal experience. It's a journey. I know: I've been there ... TWICE.

The frightening, frustrating and frantic pace of studying for the Graduate Management Admissions Test (GMAT), evaluating if the Graduate Record Exam (GRE) is a better option for you, and figuring out how to verbalize your short-term and long-term goals can create such overwhelming self-doubt that it has the potential to make you crumble. Applying to business school is hard. And, to add to the stress level, there are various challenges that first generation MBA applicants need to understand so you can be competitive as you apply to the Top 10, Top 15 or Top 25 MBA programs in the nation. However, it can be done and it does get done: Every year, people like you are getting it done! Just follow the roadmap you created for yourself!

For the overwhelming majority of business school applicants who are not first generation applicants, the concept of graduate school is a not a new phenomenon within their households. Their parents, or their grandparents have had an awareness of what an advanced degree is and the benefits it can provide. Many have graduate degrees themselves, so motivating their children to think beyond college has always been normal. However, others whose parents are the backbone of the blue-collar economy or who come from families that have not yet had a family member pursue an advanced degree are the first generation applicant. So how is it different? The application is the same, the requirements are the same, and GMAT/GRE test is the same, so what are the additional challenges? In my opinion, here are the Top 5 challenges that I have seen with first generation MBA applicants.

Top 5 Challenges of First Generation MBA Applicants

1. Possessing the Ability to Sell Yourself

Coming from humble beginnings teaches you how to be humble. Growing up, we are taught not to rock the boat, be loyal, work hard and things will fall into place.

In business, you have to be polished, ready to compete and to humbly brag about your accomplishments. So how do you develop this skill in a short time to be successful in a business school program? You Practice! Practice saying out loud why you want an MBA. Practice saying out loud why your No. 1 school is your No. 1 school. Does the MBA program have a curriculum that screams your name? Does it have a student culture that just fits perfectly with your personality? If so, practice saying why you feel passionately about that school and practice saying why you are a good fit to be there, too. Talk about the contributions you can make to the program. Share your leadership stories, either at work, or with your fraternity/sorority/ or volunteer work. Sell the school on why you will be a great choice to join their incoming class.

2. Overcoming Your Mental Block That You Are Not Good Enough

There are three simple rules in life:

- *If you do not go after what you want, you will never have it*
- *If you do not ask, the answer will always be no*
- *If you do not step forward, you will always be in the same place*

In the past ten years, I have spoken with, interviewed, and coached more than 1,000 first generation MBA applicants. The self-imposed mental block many expressed on why they believed they were not ready to compete at the highest academic levels is disheartening. The majority of the MBA candidates who choose to limit their scope of prospective business schools usually say it's because of family reasons. I am not referring to those applicants who are married and must limit their choice of schools because their spouse has a great job and it does not make financial sense to move. I am, however, referring to those who just do not want to leave the safety of the nest because they don't believe they can compete, because of circumstances beyond their control.

When applicants ask me how many business schools they should apply to, I always say to apply to no more than five MBA programs. Applying to five programs forces you to have discipline and to be strategic about where you want to be. It forces you to evaluate your strengths, your areas of improvement and decide which schools you will be competitive when submitting your application. Five is a good number because it will still afford you the opportunity to apply to one or two aspirational programs.

If you aspire to be a business leader – and through your own work experiences – you already know that a manager must set objectives in order for their team to achieve success. If your manager gave you 15 different goals that you had to excel in, you wouldn't know where to begin. Applying to business school is similar. By limiting your pool to five schools, not only are you creating a more manageable goal for yourself, you can allow yourself to aim high at one or two schools and truly give it your best effort.

As for those who do not want to leave the nest, unless there are several Top 25 MBA programs in your city, you are harming yourself in the long run if you do not at least try to get into a top MBA program. Just because you apply does not mean you have to attend the program. Give yourself the opportunity to have choices, and if you get in, maybe there will be some scholarship money with the acceptance letter and that will help make your decision a bit easier.

3. Ability to Write Out Your Career Goals

Writing is a lost art. For many first generation MBA applicants, a degree of writer's block seems to occur. From my experience, frustration sets in too early in the writing process and some choose to stop the application process completely because they cannot move beyond the first essay question. The easiest way to approach your business school application essays is by telling a memorable story. As first generation MBA applicants, you have many stories that you can share about your families and how you grew up. These stories form the core of why you will be a competitive force in business. The only part that will require time is crafting your story in an essay format.

The worst thing you can do is get stuck and stop. Keep writing and something great will eventually come out.

4: Getting a Letter of Recommendation

This is where we talk about the dreaded ASK! You need to ask your manager for a letter of recommendation without feeling guilty that you may quit your job or will be disappointing your boss. Unless you are working in a family business, your boss probably already knows that she/he will not keep you forever. So taking a proactive approach to ask for their support in your effort to apply to business school is most likely a request that your boss was already expecting.

Nevertheless, even when we do build up the courage to ask for a letter of recommendation, we hardly ever get involved with the drafting of the letter. Provide your recommender with the questions that the schools are asking. Give your recommender time to think how they will answer the question. Invite them to lunch/coffee or a walk so you can both brainstorm on which examples to give to ensure the letter of recommendation will be solid. Make sure your recommender has a clear understanding where you see your career progressing. Give your recommender the deadlines when each letter of recommendation is due. By being involved, you will reduce your stress level and will be helping your recommender to provide you with his or hers best work.

5. Relying on Your Circle of Friends to Proofread Your Essays

Having a close network of friends who you can share life experiences with is essential to your personal development and happiness. However, asking your peer group to provide you with a critical review of your essays is not the best approach on how to improve your story. Business schools ask varying questions in order to get the most insight from their applicants.

For example,

- Stanford asks, "What Matters Most to You, and Why?"
- Duke asks, "Share with us your list of '25 Random Things' about YOU"
- Cornell asks, "You are the author for the book of Your Life Story. Please create the table of contents for your book."

Unless your friends have demonstrated a proven track record to successfully coach individuals on how to address these types of essay questions, you are doing yourself a disservice by asking them to proofread and provide you guidance. Reach out to current students, recent alumni, or hire an MBA Admissions consultant to help you navigate through this journey.

The challenges for first generation MBA applicants are unique. You are expected to perform at equal or higher levels than your peers who may have had years of mental preparation. The task is not insurmountable. Many have successfully accomplished their goals, but success is seldom achieved alone. Ask for help. Lean on those who are willing to give you their time to provide you with the necessary assistance. Create an action plan and earn your MBA!

CHAPTER 2

Passionate about Education

• • •

My passion for the topics on Education and Career Success runs deep because I believe we do not always compete for success when we are at our strongest. Frequently, I see that we pursue change when we are at low points. Some change jobs because they are unhappy, not because they want a new or bigger career challenge. Some leave school because they are unhappy, instead of perhaps transferring and searching for a new environment where they can flourish. Others dedicate their lives to serve communities before they themselves have been fully served and empowered to give back with financial might. These decisions limit your ability to negotiate because you do not have a better alternative. In the world of business, leverage is a powerful tool. You cannot negotiate salary without a competing offer, you cannot ask for additional financial aid without a better financial aid package somewhere else, and you cannot empower the community if the community does not believe you have the ability to empower. While I fully understand life and the reasons why someone will need to make a move now versus later, it does not mean that the decision to make a move was the right choice. We as a people have endured many things and, while frustrating at times, focusing on your education and career must be a priority.

While no one wants to hear a "we were so poor" story, there is a sense of empowerment and camaraderie when we know that our backgrounds and challenges are similar and yet, success was still attained. I want to share more of my story with you to illustrate why I share my mindset to focus on education and career.

My life was very different from that of my parents. My childhood was spent in South-Central Los Angeles, which was a complex place to live. I wasn't far from Watts – close to Compton – and police car sirens were an everyday affair, ambulances racing through the streets were typical and the frequency of helicopters flying above us during the day or night was normal. Growing up, I viewed South-Central L.A. as simply home.

My parents and I lived in a small house. It was only 600 square feet or so. While today there are hit TV shows on "tiny homes," I lived that life for 20 years and it was never glamorous. Our house was what I would call one- and-a-half bedrooms. I say "half" because it wasn't until I was older, when I went away for school, and saw how others around the country lived did I really understand the small footprint of our home. There was the living room, where most of the family spent our time. Beyond that, there was a bedroom. The bedroom wasn't very big, but it was a bedroom. On the other side of the bedroom was a tiny space that could just fit a twin-size bed – that's what I consider to be the "half." When I was growing up with my sister, we didn't know how small the space really was – that the little room wasn't really a bedroom so much as an extra space.

There were no doors on the rooms, and to get to the small room, we had to pass through the actual bedroom. There was little privacy in the space because it was both open and cramped. It was a very different picture of normal than a lot of other people were used to, but it was what we had at the time. My parents had put so much into simply making the journey to a new country that even a small home in California was better than being in El Salvador.

Their sacrifice didn't stop with the trip across the border. Even in our home, they put my sister and me first. We were given the middle bedroom for our space – a set of bunk beds were erected to make more room and maximize on the limited space that actually existed. My mother slept in the living room, setting up space on the sofa bed at the end of the day once we were tucked in. My father slept in the tiny alcove on the twin-sized bed.

Imagine today if you slept on the opposite sides of the house from your spouse/partner, with your kids between you. That was our home for twenty years. My parents had done so much before we were even born – traveling from their home country to a brand new one – and it didn't stop there. When there wasn't room for them to even share a bed, they simply did what they had to do to make sure we were taken care of. My parent – and most parents – were singularly focused on making sure they were giving their children a better life.

As a typical Latino kid, I was living the dual life of speaking English in school to my teachers and coming home to speak Spanish and help my parents navigate American culture. My parents were vocal about the importance of an education – they wanted me to make something of myself, and knew school was the way to make that happen.

Outside of the four walls of our home, my section of Los Angeles was a turbulent place. There were neighborhoods that were rougher than others, riddled with theft and crime. There was a prevailing idea that if you went to school in those areas you were destined to find yourself on the street, with a gun, being part of the problem. The reality was that not everyone from the neighborhood fell victim to it. Some of us rose beyond it to achieve different things with our lives, but it wasn't easy. It would have been much easier to fall prey to the stereotypical idea of South-Central LA, however, my parents wouldn't have that – they wanted me to get an education. From a young age, I knew that was important to them, and I wanted to be able to make them proud. They worked hard for my sister and me and what they wanted in return was for us to focus on school, work hard, and establish successful careers.

My sister and I were on lock-down growing up. We left the house to go to school, and we would come home and do our homework. Our free time was spent studying. My mother and father knew that if they didn't hold us accountable to that, there would be other distractions that could have negatively influenced us.

I took karate and swimming down at the local YMCA, but my mother walked me to and from, each time. We didn't go to birthday parties, or hang out at the mall. It was a life completely focused on the home and doing schoolwork. The most freedom I had was riding my bike up and down my block – and that was it. I was literally confined to the block. It can be easy to make fun of the "tiger moms" out there, but when you've moved to a new country for a better chance for your child, you understand how important it is to keep them focused and safe.

At the time, it may have felt restrictive, but in hindsight, I would probably have done the same thing. Even for being new to the country, my parents knew there were better schools for me to be attending. The disparity between private and public schools was extreme, and the reality was that to attend private school, my parents would have to make a lot more money than they did. My father was the sole provider and his annual salary was $16,000. Attending private school was not within the realm of affordability.

My parents were never able to fully learn the English language. Living in Los Angeles allowed them to live life in Spanish, but even with their limited language capabilities, they knew that my attending my neighborhood schools would not be their first choice. So my mother asked my sixth grade teacher for the best junior high school in the area, and she recommend a school with a unique program that focused on high-achieving students. This was 1986, and the beginning of developing a hybrid of a charter school inside of a public school. The program was innovative, young, and small – and it was perfect for me. All students were required to pass an entrance exam, interview, and submit a letter of recommendation from your teacher. Although the junior high school was public, it required extra effort to be selected. This was the beginning of me breaking through.

When I was in the seventh grade, I had a counselor who saw potential in me. She was the one who had the first vision of me really taking my education to a higher lever and accomplishing something bigger on a national scale. Prep school was where she wanted to see me end up, and prep school was an entirely different world than I was used to. She said she saw my potential and wanted to groom me for success in that arena. I did not truly understand the concept of prep school because as it was explained to me, it's a high school where you live on campus, or in other words, boarding school. My parents trusted my counselor and I had faith in what she was saying, so I followed her wisdom and implemented her advice. She gave me a roadmap and I followed it with confidence. The roadmap was thorough, and it focused was on being a well-rounded student. Earning strong grades is expected, but demonstrating your leadership skills is what sets you apart. My counselor encourage me to be active outside the classroom and to seek leadership roles within every organization in which I was involved.

In an effort to demonstrate my academic abilities, I was a two-time participant in our school's competitive academic pentathlon team. If you are not familiar with this concept, think of Olympic Decathlon where athletes compete in 10 different categories. Our academic pentathlon team consisted of 7 members and we took exams in 5 subjects competing against dozens of other schools. The team that scored the most points across the five subjects was deemed the winner. This made me different. I was also Vice President of Student Government Club, President of our Campus Beautification Club, member of the Drama Club, and a three time first-place winner in our school's annual oratory contests. My roadmap was to showcase my skills outside of earning strong grades and to prove that I could handle multiple extra-curricular activities and perform at a high level. I did this between the ages of 13-15, and this template become the roadmap that I have implemented at every stage of my academic and professional life when I needed to further strengthen my personal brand. Whether it was excelling in school or at work, I wanted everyone to know that I could contribute more, without hampering my expected responsibilities, and to perceive me as an effective leader.

So, as I applied to prep school, I had no idea what criteria they used to evaluate prospective students. Moreover, as a child of immigrants, the whole idea of prep schools was foreign to me. Without somebody advocating for you and giving you guidance, there's no way to be successful on your own. My counselor back then knew what I would need to do to be attractive to the selective schools and worked on making me a competitive candidate. She gave me the roadmap.

She got me involved in student government so that I could have experience as a leader. She challenged me to push myself. I began tutoring younger students, and working on public speaking. She pushed me at school the way that my parents pushed me at home. I had to learn how to flourish. I set myself apart from the competition in my school by delivering a speech to the Los Angeles school board, creating a club to keep the school clean and positioning myself top of mind whenever the school needed volunteers. She tailored my experience to be exactly what would make me competitive as I applied for admission. While I was only 15 years old, I had not yet developed the vision to foresee that admission to prep school would change the trajectory of my life.

This is the story I share with parents when they ask me how they can support their children in school. I stress that leadership comes in many styles but there is no substitute to being the first to say yes to a volunteer opportunity.

My parents agreed with my counselor, and when it was time for me to apply to prep school, we worked hard as a family on my application to attend prep school. Paying tuition was something my father just could not do and – although we were excited with the idea of what could be – we also knew that finances could damper my ambition. Nevertheless, I had my eyes on the prize, so I applied for a scholarship.

A few months after I submitted my application, I had heard from my dream school. I had been accepted to Phillips Exeter Academy, a boarding school in New Hampshire. It was such an honor and it felt unbelievable. I had been competing against a lot of other highly qualified students across the country for those spots in school. The fact that I got in was amazing, and it was life-altering. I had been given the door to a different opportunity academically and socially. Looking back, without my counselor taking the time to coach me on how to be a strong candidate, my admission never would have happened. Because of her love and mentorship, I had broken through one of the challenges of growing up in a place like South-Central Los Angeles.

A New World

At 15, I flew across the country by myself to attend school in New Hampshire. Unlike my parents who had journeyed far in the trunk of a car, my life was already easier. Prep school was an entirely different world than South-Central LA, and I was dropped into it by myself. Kids knew that I was there on scholarship, but so were a few others. We all worked hard at our studies, but it was apparent who had gotten there because that school experience was bred into their family line.

While the school work did not come easy to me, and I had my academic struggles there, my biggest challenge was learning how to live far from home. I had to figure out how to become self-reliant when my family's emotional support was not readily available. In my new world, I was academically weak, but I had to become emotionally strong. I had no other choice, because my alternative was to fail. I can pinpoint to this experience as to where my resilience began to develop and I have carried this strength throughout every stage of my life.

Like my life at home, life at boarding school revolved around work. In California, I didn't want to disappoint my parents. In New Hampshire, the focus was not getting kicked out of boarding school due to low academic performance. I did not possess brut, raw intelligence, but I found ways to stick around. I knew the spot I had was hard to come by, and that lots of people had fought for it before it was given to me. Losing it would have been disheartening to my family, my counselor, and myself. Failure was not an option. Similar to my parents finding a way to survive, I took channeled that energy to make sure I achieved my goal to graduate.

After Phillips Exeter, I was accepted to Syracuse University. My parents were thrilled because their dream of having an American born, college-educated son was becoming realized. I too was thrilled! It was something that never would have been possible without all the steps along the way. My parents had sacrificed so hard for this and never let me quit.

There has always been a challenge for me to prove myself again – whether it was getting a scholarship to boarding school, or getting into a good college. Little did I know that this experience of "proving yourself" would become the foundation to what creates a polished persona. Learning how to deal with questions, perceptions, attitudes, and misconceptions is what leaders do. It builds your character. As Latinos, we need to learn how to deal with this reality and enhance our leadership skills. After college, Syracuse opened the door for me to earn a job in financial services. Almost five years later, I decided to go back to school and earn my MBA at Georgetown University, which was an honor and a new challenge. Attending a nationally recognized business school is an accomplishment, and the nature of business means that the students are competitors, which is a good thing. However, there will always be scenarios where some excel in life not because of their intellectual ability, but rather because of their connections. Frankly, we as a community need to accept that fact and embrace it. It happens, it has always happened and it will continue to happen. What you need to do is network and create your own circle of connections. My advice is, be unapologetic with the connections that you build or those that others have built for you. While some may become envious of opportunities that may be presented to you, you keep moving forward.

While I was in business school, many of the Latinos were members of the National Society of Hispanic MBAs (now called Prospanica). This association hosts an annual conference where many Fortune 500 companies come together at a career fair to recruit top talent. It was not a stretch to foresee that several of my classmates would receive job offers from this conference, however, what was hard to foresee were the envious comments made that jobs were solely offered because they happened to be Latino. I heard comments often made about the jobs that were reserved for minorities – members of the majority culture commenting on how they felt hindered and held back when a minority student got into a program or was given a job that was set aside to equalize the makeup of the student body. It can be disheartening to hear that you do not belong where you are, and that is one of the primary challenges of growing up an immigrant in America, but recognize that fact and Rise Up anyway!

As Latinos, we need to be ready for opportunity. Doors open and close, and many will remain closed. Our culture is based on three simple attributes: Strength, Struggle and Sacrifice. This is what we know and this is what we will continue to do. There is rarely anything worth having that comes easy. For certain people, that path is even more challenging. The key is to not be discouraged by the doors that close all around you, but rather to be keenly focused on the one that opens. That's the door that you need to propel yourself through to be successful.

Tons of opportunities are missed by those who expect things to be handed to them. Never expect something to be handed to you. The challenge is to recognize what you want, identify what you need to get there, and to hit the ground running.

That's the key when it comes to success in a world where you are new to the culture, or have family that doesn't understand the system. Ultimately, there needs to be someone to advocate and fight for the opportunities that are out there. Success is seldom achieved alone – you don't know what you don't know and without someone pointing you in the right direction, it's nearly impossible not to get lost along the way. I share my story with you to emphasize that my beginning is your beginning and that following a roadmap is your way to get ahead too.

The Misconception with College Admissions

One of the biggest misconcpetions is that once we get to college, we have made it. I frown on that belief because, in my opinion, that is when we need the most support. Up until college, we lived in one world – our respective neighborhoods. While the neighborhood might have been poor, crime-ridden, and challenging, we learned how to navigate around it. However, once you get to college, you will see the clashing of worlds coming together.

You will be expected to interact with people who have nothing in common with you, can arguably possess better academic foundations then you, may be more financially stable than you, yet you must still perform well academically. You will be expected to understand their world, and not much will be expected from them to understand your world. You will go from a school community that looked a lot like you to a school community were you are now truly the minority.

College is not the finish line, rather, it symbolizes where the game begins. Offices of Student Affairs, Multicultral Affairs, and other on campus resources can help first generation students like you transition as smooth as possible, but the expectation will be that you stay afloat and do well. There will be a learning curve, and after your first year or two, you will have adjusted to college life. However, the largest disparity will come when your classmates whose families have already networked for their children help them get summer internships or jobs after college, and your family may not be in a posiotion to help you brainstorm on how to secure your first job. That difference, multiplied by every other Latino graduate across the country, will create the income gap between us and them. While we are pursuing careers in social work or other entry level positions, your classmate will somehow have secured a job on Wall Street, consulting, marketing or perhaps even being admitted to a highly prestigious graduate school. So, though your family may not be able to give you suggestions on how to graduate from college with options, I will. Here is the roadmap that I want you to consider following.

Graduating from College with Options

As you come to accept that there will be life after college, you must begin thinking toward the future. Some of you may be planning to go on to graduate school while others may be ready to take on the world and get your first job! Whether you are applying for graduate school or a job, there are specific items you should focus on in order to start your life after college off successfully.

Typically, when I'm working with MBA applicants, I tell them that there are six focus factors. If the track you're on is to get your first job, the last factor won't apply to you today. However, that doesn't mean you won't decide to pursue a graduate degree sometime in the future!

The six focus factors include Essays, Work Experience, the Interview, Letters of Recommendation, your GPA, and, if you're going on to graduate school, your Graduate Records Examination (GRE), Graduate Management Admission Test (GMAT) or other graduate school entrance examination. Each of these items is important – and daunting – and every applicant has to make his or her way through them.

Sometimes it's helpful to think of the factors in terms of their Qualitative and Quantitative features. The Quantitative factors are your grade point average and test scores. These factors are set in stone and are representative of your performance. The Qualitative factors are the essays, work experience, interview, and letters of recommendation. These are the factors that you have the ability to craft. You can use them to tell your story and to highlight your ability to overcome challenges.

Most of us don't have a spotless record. I'll bet you've got a semester or two that you wish you'd studied a bit more diligently. Maybe something happened in your personal life that sidetracked you for a period of time and your grades weren't up to your usual standards. Regardless, imperfection is not a reason to give up on the dreams you have for your future. So let's take each focus factor, one at a time, and get ourselves on the right track!

Focus Factor 1: Personal Essays

You have total control of two areas when it comes to a graduate school or job application: your essay and your personal interview. In the case of a job search, the tips for your personal essay will apply to your cover letter. Let's start by considering how you can develop an effective essay.

These five steps to creating an essay or cover letter will help you make a great first impression.

1. Define your theme.
2. Be organized.
3. Tell a compelling story.
4. State goals clearly.
5. Finish strong.

Define Your Theme

In the case of a personal essay or cover letter, you need to focus on telling the reader exactly who you are. Every person has a unique selling proposition – something that sets you apart and makes you stand above the crowd. Consider all of your achievements and ask yourself, "Where do my passions lie? What things am I most proud of?" Everyone has a unique story to tell about what makes him or her special and will make him or her a valuable part of a graduate program or business team.

Be Organized

Before you sit down with your computer and start writing, consider how to organize your essay or cover letter. If it's disorganized and difficult to follow, the reader – an admissions officer or hiring authority – will stop reading and move on to the next person's essay. You want to consider how you'll start and finish your essay or cover letter, as well as what points you want to cover in between. You cannot submit a novel, so use an economy of words, and craft each sentence so that it delivers a clear message.

Tell a Compelling Story

Individuals in the position of hiring employees or reviewing admissions applications read hundreds of letters and essays. You want yours to be memorable in a good way. Consider your past work or volunteer experience. When have you shown you are a leader? What is something you can point to as a unique achievement that a reader will remember? Make a connection with the reader. Whether its an essay or cover letter, this is your personal brand that the reader must clearly see and believe that you will be an asset to the company or the graduate program. Your story is what makes you different. This is not the time to be humble. As a culture, we frown on highlighting too much on our achievements. You are competing for a job or a seat to a selective graduate program. You need to share your successes!

State Goals Clearly

Before you can start writing a personal essay or cover letter you need to know what your short- and long-term goals are and be able to express them confidently. Know how this job or degree will help you reach a career goal. And keep in mind that even if you aren't sure about your 10-year goal, set one now, knowing that it can be changed, and then be confident when you communicate that goal. The purpose of the exercise is to demonstrate that you have a vision for your yourself. Even if you are struggling on the inside aned not quite sure it, on the outside, portray that you have a path you are following. You will always be able to change direction, but to be competitive, you need to demonstrate that you have clearly defined goals and you are an individual who is well poisitioned to achieve those goals

Finish Strong

The last paragraph of your essay or cover letter is the last thought you'll be leaving a potential employer or admissions counselor to mull over. In many ways it's the most important paragraph because it's the place where you tie every point you've made together into a final thought. This isn't the place to introduce a new idea or tell a new story. This is the place where you highlight the most important ideas and tell the reader how that will benefit their organization. This is your final opportunity to be memorable.

Bonus! A Golden Nugget

If you're finding it difficult to put your finger on your unique selling proposition, here are a few tips to help you!

- Think Leadership – Just because you didn't have a leader's title doesn't mean you weren't a leader.
- Tell Your Story.
- Provide specific examples of accomplishments. Make note of your perseverance.
- Showcase your ability to overcome challenges.
- Recall times when you were forced to overcome adversity.

Focus Factor 2: Work Experience

You're not going to work for JP Morgan Chase or Citi Bank while you're a freshman in college and you probably aren't going to be offered the corner office and a six-figure salary when you land your first job. The world doesn't work that way.

Most of us begin our careers by working jobs that aren't glamorous. However, they provide the opportunity to learn and demonstrate a strong work ethic. If you work hard and show that you are a team player, you will move up. This is how careers begin.

So what should you do to highlight your work and/or volunteer experience? Here are three main elements you should highlight:

- You are a team player.
- Your work experience has progressed over time.
- How you stand out from the crowd.

A Team Player

When you're describing your work experience, it is just as important to show how you work with others as it is to detail your responsibilities. Discuss the experiences you had with a particular company and try to illustrate how you worked with your team effectively. Are you a strong team player? Point out that you can lead and you can follow. Let them know through examples that you're willing to step up to be a leader if the situation calls for it or that you recognized that for a specific situation, you contributions were best served playing a supporting role to help the team leader implement his or her ideas. Not everyone can be the "chief" all the time, but you can illustrative your versatility and willingness to help the team achieve their goal by demonstrative your positive "team focused" attitude.

Show a Progression

This can be tricky early in your career or if you've not had many jobs. However, do what you can to show an upward progression. If you worked mowing lawns for a landscaping company in high school, but ended up selling contracts for lawn service to new clients, that's an upward progression. If you are writing your cover letter, and you had a summer internship, briefly write about your experience and how you used that as a springboard to get your first full-time job after college. As long as you have upward movement, you are on a good track. It's also important to describe how you achieved the upward progression. Did you begin selling new services to clients on your own? Did you ask for additional responsibility? Either answer is a good one and demonstrates something important about what you bring to a graduate program or job.

How Do You Stand Out?

When you're detailing your work experience, make special note of how you differed (in a positive way) from your co-workers. Are you particularly good at organizing complex projects? Are you naturally good at customer service? Are you a problem solver? Dig deep and, if you're not sure how you're different, consider asking your manager or a co-worker. Sometimes an alternate perspective is all it takes to shed a little light on what makes you stand out from the crowd.

Bonus! A Golden Nugget

Are you still scratching your head and wondering what you should include to help you stand out in the crowd?

- Highlight team accomplishments. How did you help your team find success?
- Include your corporate awards and recognition.
- Discuss how you balance work responsibilities with community service activities.

Focus Factor 3: The Interview

You have more control over your success during an interview than you think. This doesn't mean that you'll be able to direct the interview. It means you will be more confident. It means you'll be able to tell your story.

The interview is a critical part of any application process. It is especially significant if you have something in your past – a low GPA or test score, for instance – that you want to address. You can show the interviewer that you are more than a collection of facts on a resume. You can make it obvious that a test score does not define you. In short, you can sell your strengths in a way that will make the interviewer look past your weaknesses.

If someone advises you to "Relax and be yourself," ignore them. You need to get ready to perform. This means several things:

- Research
- Prepare
- Practice
- Execute

Research

By the time you reach a job or admissions interview, you should know your own strengths and weaknesses. You need to know everything you can about the company or school that will be interviewing you. You also need to know everything about the schools or businesses with whom they compete.

If you are interviewing for a job, know the job description well. What can you find out about the person who will be interviewing you? What is the corporate culture? Know what skills you have that make you the perfect candidate. Also, know the possible career paths so that you can speak to how you can grow with the organization.

If you're interviewing for admission to a graduate school, know why that school is the best one for you. Research the graduate program and know what sets it apart. Is there a particular professor who heads the department? Does the program offer courses that aren't offered elsewhere?

Prepare

Preparation is the key to feeling confident in your interview. You've done the research; now start thinking about the interview itself. Write down a list of possible questions and write out your answers. Construct your answers with an introduction, a body, and a conclusion that relates to the program or job. How will you address the question? What story about yourself can you share that will help answer the question? How will you highlight your ability to lead and be a good team member?

Whether your interview is academic or career related, you can be sure you'll have to answer at least the four most common questions.

1. *What are your strengths and weaknesses?*
2. *What are your goals? Short term? Long term?*
3. *Why this school/company? Why now?*
4. *Tell me about yourself.*

These questions should be the easiest for you to answer. You are answering questions that will let the interviewer get to know you. As you construct your answers on paper, remember that you are writing your own story.

It is necessary to be candid about your history. An easy thing to do when you're talking about your successes. What about when the interviewer asks you about weaknesses or failures? The wrong answer is, "I don't fail." An interviewer knows that answer is either a lie or it's the truth indicating you refuse to take any risks or step outside of your comfort zone. Neither of these are messages you want to send. A weakness or a mistake is not failure. Failure is refusing to make mistakes so you can grow.

Consider your experience, goals, and ambitions. Tell the interviewer not just about your work and school history but about what is important to you. Do you volunteer? What makes you well-rounded? Tell the interviewer what makes you a valuable asset. Highlight your accomplishments, your ability to overcome adversity, and your unique selling proposition.

Practice

The worst thing any candidate can do is become a rambler. During interviews, the simple concept of "less is more" is best. That's one of the reasons you should write down answers to the questions you know you'll be asked.

Find someone you trust to give you constructive feedback and then role-play. When you role-play, have them ask you a question and then, before you give your answer, repeat the question. Then give your answer using the introduction, body, and conclusion you wrote out. Always remember that your answer must tie back into whatever position or program you're interviewing for.

Here is an example:

Interviewer: Tell me about a time when you reached a goal despite a challenge.
Applicant: I'd be happy to tell you about a time when I reached a goal despite a challenge. I want to talk to you about the time that

my job was to put up flyers around campus to promote one of my club's on-campus events. I had fifty-five flyers to put up. Very limited. Our budget didn't go very far. Nevertheless, I knew the seven buildings that the students traveled to the most on campus. Each building was between two and three stories. I chose to put them in the café, the entrance, and in the student areas where I knew people would congregate. Therefore, even though I had fifty-five flyers, I was able to effectively market our event by positioning our message in areas where I knew there was high exposure. In addition, I can do the same thing for you. My natural creativity and strong work ethic helps me deliver results on very little money or sometimes no money but just pure sweat equity. I can bring that passion and perseverance to your company and help you find a creative way to tackle the markets that may be forgotten but are still profitable.

Your goal is to have this kind of response for every question you can anticipate. Have the person who is helping you role-play also help you brainstorm. They have a different perspective and may naturally have a follow-up question or want additional information. Add these questions to your prepared list and create answers. Role-playing, while sometimes a little awkward, will help you to feel less awkward and nervous in the interview.

Bonus! A Golden Nugget

When you're researching and preparing your answers, be sure to consider the following:

- What is the school or company culture? Talk to others who work or study there. Look online for any information that might be available.
- Speak about why you see that school or organization to be essential to achieve your goals.

- How will you contribute to the program, classroom, organization, company or department?
- How is your unique skill set a valuable asset to the company or school?
- What community service have you done? How is that important to who you are as a person and candidate?
- When you are creating your answers, remember that sometimes the right answer isn't about "I" but about "we." How have you been a team player?
- Whether you're interviewing for a graduate program or a job, always sell that you are a leader. While "we" is important, don't let your humility humble you too much were you are not demonstrating your contributions.

Execute

You may not have the best grades. You may not have had a job where you were able to carry the title of manager. Your history may have a blemish or two in it. However, in your interview, your job is to make sure none of those things matter. Using your well-prepared answers, smile, look your interviewer in the eye, and tell them why you are so much more than your grades or your mistakes. Tell them why you are an asset and a leader.

You've done all the preparation and practice. You've left no stone unturned in your research. Now is the time to execute.

Focus Factor 4: Letters of Recommendation

Throughout your life, you're going to need letters of recommendation. You'll need them to get jobs. You'll need them to get into graduate school. So how do you make sure you're getting good recommendations from the right people?

- Foster relationships with your professors or managers.
- Consider what you'll need based on your future goals.
- Be thoughtful about how you ask for a letter of recommendation.

Foster Relationships

Not only will it be uncomfortable to ask, but also you probably won't get a very good recommendation from a professor who only knows you through your test scores and term papers. Think about all of the professors you know and then ask yourself, "Whom do/did I look up to?" How much contact did I have with that professor? How well do they know me?"

Decide which professors you would like to ask for a letter of recommendation and then do what you can to get to know them. Become a familiar face they see in the front row participating. Stop by their office during office hours to discuss course-related information. Ask them for advice about your future. Let them know who you are. Don't be a pest, but do show up. You are not stalking, but rather, you are making your presence known.

The same ideas apply to managers at your job – even if it's work study or part-time. Those people see a different side of you. They see how you interact with customers or notice that you'll stay late to be sure everything is done. Those are important points-of-view. Get to know your managers in an appropriate way. Look to them for guidance.

Consider Your Needs

What do you want your letter of recommendation to say? Do you want it to highlight your work ethic? Do you want to emphasize your experience helping a professor with research? Do you want to talk about your willingness to volunteer time for a special project or to tutor classmates?

What do you need it to say? If you're applying for a job, you need your letter to mention your leadership abilities, ability to persevere, willingness to work as part of a team. You need your letter of recommendation to tell prospective employers what makes you the best candidate for their open position.

If you're applying to graduate school, it's also important for letters to highlight your leadership and team skills. However, you also want it to address academics. How are your grades? Are you a great writer? Do you have innovative problem-solving skills? Are you the kind of person who won't accept less than the best from yourself? Were you involved with extra-curricular activities that shaped who you are today?

Be Thoughtful

Your professors and managers are busy people. When you ask them for a letter of recommendation be sure to provide them with the information they need. Should it be addressed to a specific school or person? Should it be a general letter or are there pre-set questions they must answer?

Every letter you request needs to come with an explanation of your needs for that letter. It isn't enough to ask, "Will you please write me a letter of recommendation?" That's too vague and may not really help you reach your goals in the end. Ask for a letter and provide the writer with a little guidance about points you'd like them to mention.

Finally, try to give them some time to write the letter. You don't want to ask for a letter of recommendation and tell them you need it the next day. Give them time to thoughtfully consider what they want/need to say and how they will say it.

Bonus! A Golden Nugget

Eight hints for how to properly ask for a letter of recommendation:

1. Write a letter thanking your recommender for investing time in your future and explain how their words will play a critical role in your success.
2. Outline your short and long-term career goals for your recommender.
3. Specify how this degree or job helps you reach your goals.
4. Tell them why that particular school's graduate program or that company is important to you.
5. Provide the deadlines for each letter.

6. Give them the questions they need to answer for you.
7. Tell them what you want them to address in those questions.
8. Share your personal reasons on what motivates you to apply for a particular job or graduate program.

Focus Factor 5: Grade Point Average

Your Grade Point Average (GPA) matters. That's obvious while you're still in college. In addition, it also helps paint the picture of who you are when you apply to graduate school or for your first job. Most applications will ask for your GPA and many people choose to put it on their resume.

If you have a high GPA, you're in great shape. This will simply be an area that a potential employer or school will check off their list. However, if you have a low GPA, they may raise an eyebrow and wonder why your GPA is low. So the question for someone with a lower GPA: How do you overcome a low GPA?

- Look for options to retake coursework.
- Boost your GPA with other courses.
- Explain.

Retake

Sometimes the best thing you can do is retake the course or two that brought your overall GPA down. You may have had difficulty keeping up in that course because you overloaded your semester. You may have had personal issues that distracted you and kept you from doing your best work. No matter the reason, retake those classes and try to improve your grade.

When you retake a course be sure you're doing it at a time that is ideal for you. If it's offered in the summer, take it then when it is the only thing you'll have to focus on. Give it 100% of your attention, look for a tutor, and make every effort to bring up your grade.

Other Coursework

This solution applies to everyone, but especially to individuals who have been out of school for a period of time and are applying for graduate school. If you're trying to compensate for a low GPA and you've been away from school for a year or two (or ten), take a few courses at a local college. Choose challenging coursework, work hard, and get top-tier grades. This allows you to point to your more recent accomplishments and say, "I know that my grades weren't fantastic when I finished college. But since then, I've taken some challenging coursework and done very well. This allowed me to prove to myself, and hopefully to you, that I'm very capable of handling graduate coursework."

Taking additional courses at a local college can also be a benefit when you're applying for a job. In this case, look for challenging courses but also look for courses that will better prepare you for a job you want. For example, maybe you'd like a job in marketing. You know that your GPA is on the low side so you take a few marketing, writing, or even design courses at your local college and do well. Now your story can be, "My GPA wasn't as good as it could have been but now that I've found a direction and a goal, I'm taking coursework to help me prepare and I'm doing very well." The entire objective here is to position your story so the person you are interacting with can see the positives.

Explain

Sometimes life gets in the way of our best intentions. It only takes a semester or two of poor grades to hurt your overall GPA. Looking back, maybe you should have taken a break from school while you were dealing with a personal problem or crisis, but you didn't. So now is the time to explain why your grades weren't what they could have been – what they would have been if you were at your best.

Perhaps you experienced the death of a loved one. In your grief, you tried to keep pressing forward. You tried to keep life "normal." However, you found that there were too many distractions from dealing with your grief, to final arrangements, and your loved one's estate. In hindsight that would have been a good semester to drop your classes but by the time you realized that, it was too late. Therefore, your grades suffered.

This is a perfectly valid reason for poor grades. Anyone would understand that you were having a difficult time and not performing at your best. Find a way to communicate your explanation for a low GPA to a potential admissions officer or employer. Look for a way to meet them in person to show them that you are a good candidate in spite of your GPA. In addition, remember to frame the story in a positive way. Let them know that you had this hardship, that it hurt your grades but that you've dealt with it and moved forward. Show them that you were able to persevere in the face of a challenge.

Focus Factor 6: Graduate Entrance Exams

Humankind has yet to create a standardized test that can measure a person's work ethic. A GMAT or GRE is only one indicator of your abilities. It tells the graduate admissions committee how well you performed on one test, on one day. So how do you overcome a less than fantastic score on your graduate entrance exam?

- Highlight your other strengths.
- Retake the test.

Highlights

You know that a test can't tell your whole story. Graduate schools know that, too. If you've taken the GMAT or GRE and your score is low, you have the ability to offset that score by highlighting your other strengths. It is as simple as addressing the score by saying, "I know that my score was low. I'm not a strong test taker. However, I have a list of achievements and recommendations that will show you who I really am. I can show you tangible evidence that proves I'm the right fit for this graduate program."

Look for, or ask for, an opportunity to explain your test scores. If you're a poor test taker or something personal kept you from doing your best on that day, ask to explain your unique circumstance. Nevertheless, be sure you aren't just making excuses. Give both the reason for a poor score as well as a list of achievements and traits that make you a suitable candidate.

Retake the Test

If you struggle with taking tests, this may not be the advice you want to hear: Retaking the test can help improve your score. If you're honest, did you truly invest the time required for you to do well? Did you take practice exams? Did you study in a way that fits your learning style?

Study better. Study more. Invest in classroom prep course designed to help you bring up your score. Unbelievably, this really works. The courses are designed to teach you not just the information you need but strategies for taking the test. Study on your own as well – especially if you learn best through books. Finally, look into online web-based adaptive courses that can help you do your best.

Everyone learns differently. Be honest with yourself about your effort. Give your very best on the second try if you didn't on the first. Explore the different methods for preparing to take the test. Choose the one the fits you best. Work hard and believe that you can bring up your score!

New Beginning

Graduating from college is both a gratifying and terrifying experience, especially if you are not sure what comes next. Graduating from college with options must be your primary objective. Whether you are applying to law school, medical school, graduate school or seeking to start your career in the real world, approaching the next chapter of your life with a proven framework is your best roadmap for success. Each focus factor provides you with a foundation that you can build on and tailor to fit your needs. Use the tips provided to you in this chapter to position yourself to receive the best options possible.

What do you do when you graduate from college without options?

Do you have FOGU? Have you heard of FOGU? I am not talking about the poisonous Japanese Puffer fish, that's *fugu*. At some point in your life, you have suffered from FOGU. FOGU stands for the Fear Of Graduating Unemployed. In the previous chapter, I shared with you detailed strategies on how to maximize your career opportunities while you are still in school. However, there is no such thing as a one-size-fits-all approach. There are many good people who unfortunately graduate from college without a job.

Graduating unemployed can be terrifying. Even with the self-preparation, the interview practicing, establishing a network, and everything in between, the possibility of graduating without a job is real. Whether you may be graduating from college or graduate school unemployed, it happens. Similar to getting laid off from work, there is a process that you must follow to secure a job and it starts with you bouncing back and reigniting your determination.

As way of illustration, I want to share with you the story of a young Latino male, Martin, whom I interviewed to help me highlight a different perspective to this real-world situation.

Martin is a mechanical engineer. He grew up in Chicago, and went to college at one of the most prestigious universities in the city of Chicago. Martin was smart, focused, lived about 15 miles away from school but decided to live on campus to truly enjoy his college experience.

Martin's Story

Man, when I graduate from college without a job I was heartbroken. I felt as if I had failed my mom. My mother was a single parent and she sacrificed hard to help pay what she could while I was in college. Going to college was both an emotional investment and achievement for our family.

I was the first in my family to go to college, but at the same time, as the first in my family, I did not know who to ask when I felt lost. My mom couldn't help because she did not understand my new world. She worked in a factory, and because of her, I wanted to become a mechanical engineer. I wanted her to say, "The boss is my son."

I was raised in a mechanical household, per se, because factories are all about machines and on the factory floor a lot of respect was given to the mechanical engineers. However, school was not easy. It was challenging because I was not truly prepared to compete on pure, raw intelligence. I was always told I was smart, but damn, some of my classmates were just next level and I struggled to keep up.

I listened to the only advice my mother knew how to give, "You need to work harder." So I worked harder.

During my junior year in college, a friend told me about the importance of getting an internship. I did not have a career counselor. While my school was prestigious, the culture was that many of my classmates already had established family connections to help secure job offers.

As an engineer, I was a member of the Society of Hispanic Professional Engineers (SHPE). Even though I was a member, I had no idea how to leverage the network. The older students would tell the newer members like myself that we should attend the career fair at the SHPE conference to help secure jobs after graduation. That sounded all good, but no one told me how. I did not know what to say. I did not know how to start a conversation or begin to express interest in a position

How do you secure a job? It's a career fair with a whole bunch of tables, booths, and people picking up flyers, trinkets and stuff from the tables. I was afraid to say hello to the recruiters. I did not know how to approach them without sounding like a fool.

What I should have done was say, "Hi, my name is Martin, and I am studying mechanical engineering here in Chicago. I am interested in learning about the entry level career opportunities at your company."

How hard is that? But even something as easy as two sentences can be terrifying if you do not know what to say or have the confidence to even speak up. That was my problem. Like a deer in the highlights, I froze. I did not yet understand the importance of making connections, developing relationships and doing what people do when they network. I was young, and had no one to coach me on how to position myself.

When I graduated from college with my degree in Mechanical Engineering, I was without a job for eight months. I was struggling. Through pure will power, I did my best to dig myself out of a hole.

While my mother was supportive, I wanted to start helping her out financially. I did not grow up with a dad, but I wanted my mother to finally feel as if she had a financially stable man of the house. So I hustled hard. Through trial and error, I figured things out. I also realized that not everyone is capable of figuring things out, which is sad.

I had friends from my neighborhood who did not go to college but could not figure out how to make things better for themselves. I wanted more and I was committed to find something. When a job opportunity came to work at the help desk of a technology company, I took the offer. I was tired of being broke so I took what was available and I approached my job with a fierce desire to excel.

It had been eight months of meeting people, developing relationships, going on interviews, just simply being aggressive and making my success my priority. Within my circle of friends, I am a talker. I am comfortable enough with them to just let loose and share my thoughts.

I learned that I needed to be more myself and when the job offer to work on the help desk came through, I was told "Listen, this is your starting point. You have the gift of gab. Help our customers with their problems, provide solutions, make them feel valued and in two to three years, you will be able to move up."

I was not looking for a job, but rather a career. I did not have time to play games, so I gladly accepted the offer and I just told myself, "I will grow from here."

Graduating from college unemployed taught me so many things about being resilient. I wish I would have had a job when I graduated because I did not want to struggle for so long, but I learned that I can overcome setbacks. I do have a happy ending I want to share with you.

After two years of working on the help desk, my manager said that they were impressed with my ability to take difficult concepts and easily explain them to our *customers over the telephone without making the customers feel less capable. He said that I have the talent to go into sales and they wanted to promote me to join the sales team.*

I thought I was an engineer, but in truth, I am an engineer who is also a problem solver and good with people. Working in sales for a tech company took me to visit clients throughout North and South America. I was flying business class, staying in 5-star hotels, and had private cars pick me up from the airport to take me to my hotel.

My mom began telling her friends that I was "el jefe" and that made me smile. In Spanish, jefe means boss. I was not el jefe – far from it – but I gave my mother a sense of pride that everything she invested in me was beginning to pay off.

After five years of working for the tech company, I decided to go back to school to earn my MBA. As with anything, I enjoyed my time but I wanted to grow even further. I had captured that corporate ambition and I wanted more. I looked at the executives from my company and most of them had MBA from top tier MBA programs. As a Latino, I was apprehensive to go down this path because, though there were a few people I knew who had MBA's, none were from top schools. However, this time, I knew how to network and began asking friends for advice on how to apply to business school.

As I made the decision to earn my MBA, I told myself that there was no way I was graduating unemployed again. My plan was to switched careers from sales to finance, and I started networking early. My school work was still important to me, but I was no longer scared of going to career conferences, such as the National Society of Hispanic MBA's and sparking up conversations with the recruiters at their tables.

I had become self-aware and self-confident. I now knew the value I was able to contribute to an organization, and I developed the courage to articulate my strengths. In essence, I had my perfect elevator pitch. From a guy who graduated from college unemployed, I graduated from business school from a Top 15 MBA program and had three job offers.

I was able to successfully switch careers and began working in New York City at a highly prestigious Investment Banking firm. While working on Wall Street does not come without its own share of corporate politics or frustration, I was able to achieve my goal to get here and that's not bad for a first generation college graduate. I learned how to bounce back, I learned how to get back up and I am moving forward.

Martin's roadmap focused on five areas:

1) Network aggressively to secure his first job after college
2) Do well at the help desk, use it as a springboard, and grow from there
3) Accept the sales promotion and serve the clients well
4) Switch careers from sales to finance and get his MBA to transition careers
5) Secure an investment banking job on Wall Street

In this case, Martin did not have his roadmap predetermined. He figured it out as he went along, but you can use this as an example as you tailor your roadmap. Understand your end goal. Envision where you want to be and work backwards to determine the major miles stones that must be achieved before you attain your goal.

The Four Types of MBA Programs:

Depending on your level of work experience, you may be considering going back to school to earn a master's degree. While I am a big believer in earning an MBA, I also recognize that not every person reading this book is necessarily MBA-minded. For the sake of illustrating a point, I will discuss the importance of evaluating four different types of MBA programs that every person should know. It is my opinion that having an MBA is an important component to achieving success in Corporate America. While you may not be ready to pursue business school, you should at least be aware of the types of MBA programs that are offered. If you are considering business school, then you may be overwhelmed by which type of MBA program is the right fit for you.

Every year, potential MBA students are debating over four types of programs: 1) Part-time, 2) Full-time, 3) Executive or 4) Online.

Part-Time

Part-time programs generally range in length from one year to three years, and students typically attend evenings and weekends on a local campus. One of the major benefits is that these programs often have reduced cost for students, as employers will offer tuition reimbursement for some of the expenses. If you enjoy working at your current employer or you are on a fast-track and know you want to stay at your employer for the mid- to long-term, a part-time program would benefit you the most. Part-time programs may be best for you if you have an obligation where your personal commitments require you to be at home.

However, if you are considering switching careers, especially if you want to switch into a traditional MBA career such as investment banking or consulting, carefully do all of your research before attending a part-time program. Generally, employers that recruit MBAs, such as the aforementioned, focus on full-time students only. Additionally, if you participate in tuition reimbursement, your employer might require two or more years of additional employment after the last payment or you will owe your employer all of the payments made on your behalf. Also, there is no opportunity for summer internship, which is crucial if you want to switch careers.

Full-Time

Full-time programs are typically one or two years in length and require students to live on or near the campus. Full-time programs are absolutely the best for someone looking to switch careers. Hundreds of employers actively recruit full-time MBA students through methods such as interviewing on campus or via national conferences. Full-time programs also offer significant opportunities to network with your classmates. If you are interested in joint-programs such as an MPH/MBA or MPP/MBA, then full-time offers the easiest opportunity.

Lastly, most of the top-ranked programs in the world offer only a full-time and executive MBA. There are a few that offer a part-time program, but by and large if you want to go to a top school you will have to go full-time.

Full-time programs, however, can be costly, with tuition and fees easily topping in the six figures. Additionally, full-time programs require you to leave your current job to attend and you will be living on savings and other financial means including loans. If you have a family, a full-time program will likely mean relocating your family while attending business school.

Executive

Executive programs are unique in that they are typically for mid-level managers with at least 10 years of work experience. Many people wrongly think that if they have been in the workforce for 10 years that automatically makes them eligible.

However, the title says executive and that is just what these programs are looking for in terms of candidates. If you have had a series of progressive promotions and/or responsibilities for at least 10 years and you are looking to become an executive, then you would be the right person for this program. Executive programs typically last one to two years with some combination of meeting virtually and then several-in person meetings lasting from a long weekend to a week. A few executive programs are even full-time on campus. This type of program is almost certainly not for people looking to switch their career or company. In many cases, the person's company nominates them and pays all of their fees since this program can be quite expensive. Most candidates view this as a way to further their career with their current employer, not to jump elsewhere.

Online

MBA programs that are online range in length from one to three years and students meet in virtual classrooms entirely online. In a few cases, there may be some limited interaction in person. The greatest benefit these programs offer is flexibility. Because the classes meet at all hours, you can easily schedule your classes for a timeframe that suits you. When considering an online program, pay attention to the school's reputation in the industry where you want to work. While no company outright bans online schools, it may be harder to explain things like team-work in an interview when you've only interacted with the other students online. In addition, research the total cost of attendance as there have been many stories in the news recently of for-profit schools that may leave students saddled with heavy debt loads and low job options compared to their peers.

The Final Choice

Before you decide what type of program to attend, it may be necessary to create a career roadmap and perform an honest examination of your career goals and personal situation. While money is a significant factor in choice, the data shows the benefits of attending a full-time program offers the best payback.

Rejected from Business School, Now What?

In the same spirit of rising up, we must also know what to do next when we fall. For many, rejection from business school is an infuriating, frustrating or even a hurtful experience. Whatever the case is, rejection is emotional. Someone said no and now you have to deal with it, but the question is HOW.

The first thing any rejected applicant must do is digest what happened. Whether yelling out loud, venting to your friends or crying in private – the first order of business is accepting the decision. Applicants are rejected for many reasons, and most of the time the reasons are valid. I have met candidates who achieved 780 GMAT scores and 3.6 GPA's but had weak essays, mediocre letters of recommendation and at that point, a rejection from business school is not hard to understand. However, the issue becomes a bit more complicated when you know in your gut you had a great interview, your essays were good and your letters of recommendation were solid. Although your GMAT score and/or GPA were borderline, you felt in your heart of hearts you had a great chance to gain admission, but now you have to deal with rejection. *Now* what!?! Well, the answer is actually easier than you may think.

Admissions committee members are people too and they are asked to determine if a borderline applicant can succeed in their program. Admission committee members are tasked with accepting a diverse, talented group of candidates that will succeed and get jobs at the end of their two years. When the applicant is truly a borderline candidate, the committee will make a judgment call and, at times, could err in judgment. This is when you, the rejected applicant, are responsible to make the committee understand that you can succeed. If you have invested the appropriate amount of face time with the admission committee, you should have a contact on the admissions committee that you can reach out to and ask for "*off the record*" feedback. If you do not have a contact, that is your first big mistake and a red flag that you did not cultivate the proper relationship to help secure an internal advocate for your borderline application.

In most cases, the reason for rejection for borderline candidates is the lack of quantitative course work or low quant percentile scores on your GMAT. This is perhaps the easiest obstacle to overcome. Ask your contact what score you need to achieve to make your application more competitive. An alternative is to take an accounting, statistics or finance class at a local community college to prove that you can handle the course work. Ask if conditional acceptance is an option. What conditional acceptance means is that you are admitted to business school but are automatically placed on academic probation. In most cases, you must maintain a 3.0 GPA during your first semester/quarter and if you do not achieve the 3.0 GPA you will be asked to leave school. Although daunting, this should be a welcomed option becomes it means you are in the school of your choice and the only thing you need to do now is prove that you can handle the workload. If you are a confident and driven applicant, this should not be a problem.

If you were successful in achieving high quant scores but still failed to gain admission, the reason then falls under three scenarios: 1) your essays were weak, 2) your recommendations were average or 3) your interview was poor. In these situations, you must take a tactical approach to your application.

Your contact should be able to give you some direction. Ask a student or alumnus from your school of choice to read your essays for feedback. If you do not have a student or alumnus to reach out to for help, then this is your second and last major red flag that you did not invest the appropriate amount of face time at the school and a rejection should no longer be a surprise to you.

However, if you do have a student to offer you feedback ask if your goals were clearly articulated, ask if you were successful in illustrating how the school will help you achieve those goals and if you demonstrated what you will contribute to the classroom. If the answer to these questions is, "not really" then you have a great opportunity to improve on your essays and reapply the following year.

While re-applicants are still measured against the same pool of candidates the following year, your application is viewed different. If you reapply, you will demonstrate the courage that you are willing to try again. However, if your application has not improved then you are wasting everyone's time and a second rejection will certainly come.

Use the feedback from the school to reassess your application. Take additional coursework to prove you can handle accounting, statistics or finance. Show how the school will position you to successfully achieve your career ambitions and more importantly, provide concrete examples how you will make the class better. Admissions committees want students who are leaders and team players. They seek students who are willing to help their fellow classmates, but are able to take command when needed.

Low GMAT scores are surmountable, but a lack of focus is not. Prove that you have vision and when you do reapply, prepare to be pleasantly surprised!

CHAPTER 3

Balancing Heritage

• • •

YOUNG LATINOS ARE FACED WITH the balancing act that comes with being born in America to immigrant parents. I had to speak Spanish at home with my family, and speak English in school. I might have watched the news in Spanish at home with my parents, but when I got to school, I also had to know the English side of things. From an early age, Latinos – children of immigrants – become responsible to hold both worlds together and make sense of it all. Experiences such as these teach us resilience, leadership, and versatility. However, on the downside, when we are unsure, afraid, or have doubt, who do we turn to? Our parents looked to us to be problem solvers, but that also makes us vulnerable when we are faced with our own issues, such as challenges at school or in our careers.

Who did you turn to when you needed academic help? For me, growing up in South-Central L.A. in the 1980s, several of my classmates were able to take their homework back to their parents and have them help them understand the assignment. My parents never learned English, so asking them for help would not provide the support I needed to succeed academically. And many Latino parents and families don't even realize that this is something that can actually set their children back from being as successful as they hope.

For me, the value in being in that situation came from learning how to ask for help. I became comfortable asking for help. My parents couldn't help me, so I had to start to identify people who could. It was the only way to stay on top of what I was doing in school, but it had a lasting effect. As

I grew up, I never had a fear of asking for help. Even as I progressed in my education and in my career, I was not afraid to admit when I did not know something and in turn, ask for help. This became my support system, circle of friends or occasional mentors. This self-awareness was my foundation to get comfortable on how to network. As I matured, I began looking for resources once I understood how leveraging opportunities could help move my ideas and me forward. This skill did not come overnight. It required work and it will require you to work too.

When we are talking about being a leader, asking for help and knowing how to build a support system is key. If you're looking to do something big, like start a business or be successful in your field – you need to ask for help. There is nothing weak about asking for it, even if you think there is sometimes. There are times when you can go for it on your own, but other times you better be ready to network and ask someone to help.

Master Networking on a Higher Level

Networking is about self-confidence. Networking is learning how to say hello to a stranger and holding a conversation. Networking is about understanding who you are, what you want to accomplish, what you can contribute to someone else and who you want to meet. Networking is about being organized, having a game plan and being prepared to share your story. Remember that you are a leader, practice articulating your examples that showcase your leadership skills and have a clear answer in case you are asked about your short-term and long-term careers goals.

To learn to network like a master, you must invest the time to practice networking at actual receptions when you do not need anything from anyone. To network effectively, you must possess the mindset that you are not speaking to people for a job, but rather engaging with someone to establish a relationship. The leverage to network like a master is that you do not come to a room from a position of weakness where you are desperately looking for your next opportunity, but rather from a position of strength where you are not looking for anything urgently, other than making new friends.

Your first attempt at networking should not be prompted because you need something and you are hoping to meet someone who can give you something. The best networkers are the ones who understand that having a circle of friends who think highly of you is valuable, so you nurture those relationships. Even more importantly, if you are a superhero for someone else because you were able to connect that individual to a different person in their time of need, your gesture will be reciprocated because needs come full circle and you will now have a friend you can lean on when you need help. Knowing how to connect with others is a trait of a master networker.

Now, let's say you actually need to network immediately and you need to learn how to network effectively quickly. If this sounds like you, here is a four-step roadmap that you can use in any networking setting.

1) Move with Purpose:
Have your game plan laid out. Your objective should not be to sniff out whoever is looking to hire. Your objective is to attend the event to establish a connection and build a relationship, not necessarily to ask for a job. Networking events are already a bit awkward and to ask for employment opportunities without someone actually knowing who you are creates an uncomfortable setting.

2) It's not about You, It's about the Connection
Your objective is to make a connection, establish a rapport, and learn how you can help each other in case they too have a need. Once the conversation is coming to a close, ask the individual if you can follow-up with them in the next day or so to continue the conversation. Don't monopolize anyone's time, and make your interaction pleasant.

3) Never Underestimate Anyone

Secretaries, Administrative Assistants and Interns have the ear of decision makers. Do not underestimate their value because of title. In many cases, their opinions carry tremendous value and if you are able to network with them, then you are on your way to become a master networker.

4) Connect Others to Each other

You might have met someone who may not be able to help you at that moment, but if you are able to connect others to people who can offer solutions it puts you in a great light. You will come across as someone who is not selfish, but rather compassionate. You cared enough about someone else to offer a solution to them. You will be viewed as a problem solver and as a great person to know.

As Latinos, culturally, we are known to be fun people. Use your natural ability, smile, and warmth to invite others into your space. Get to know others and let them get to know you. Networking is not about putting yourself in embarrassing situation where you do not know what to say. Networking is about sharing your story, having a conversation, and setting a time to reconnect in the near future. Ultimately, it is not that hard to do. You only need to build up enough courage to say, "Hello," introduce yourself and ask for their name. The rest of the conversation will fall into place.

Your effectiveness at network will also determine how quickly you rise up in Corporate America.

How to Network Within the Workplace

Networking is not always about connecting with people from outside companies. You can also connect with people who also work at your same company and you do this so you can get to know your colleagues or decision-makers better. The purpose here is to further strengthen your circle of friends. Engage with folks, have small talk, and do not hesitate to send a blind email if you want to get to know someone.

I want to share this example with you. I was coaching a young Latina, 26 years old, and she has been working at her current company for five years. Her first exposure to Corporate America was as a temporary employee working in the collections department at a major Fortune 100 company. Prior to getting hired as a temp, her ambition was to work for a large firm. Even as a temp, this young lady was grateful for the opportunity because it got her foot in the door and would also lead to full-time employment. Within six months, she was offered full-time employment, but still working in collections. For anyone who has worked in collections, these type of jobs are referred to as "Dialing for Dollars." As her time with the company progressed, she saw other folks earn promotions and leave the collections department and she began to grow frustrated because no one was acknowledging her contributions.

This is an example of the Latino work ethic, "work hard and they will notice." Unfortunately, in today's business environment, you must make yourself noticeable. You must take ownership of your own career and make strides to get on a decision maker's radar. To this young woman's credit, she reached out to me for career advice and the first thing I asked her was, "Does your boss' boss know what you want to do?" She was stunned because she never thought about reaching out a level above her boss. She felt that would be disrespectful to her boss. I challenged her on that notion because there is nothing disrespectful about getting to know how a team leader became a manager or how a manger eventually became a senior executive.

My position here is simple, YOU ARE NETWORKING! Remember, it's not about you, it's about them. After a long conversation, I told this young woman, "Email your boss' boss. Tell him that you heard that he has had a rich career within the company and that you are interested in learning more about his career path. Ask him if he will spend 20 minutes with you to share his experience on how he navigated his career." Within two hours, this young woman received a reply and the 20 minute ask was converted into a one-hour lunch session where the manager spent quality one-on-one time with her and then asked where she wanted to take her career. At the end of their lunch conversation, this young woman was on the radar and had been provided a roadmap by her boss' boss on how to pursue her career in the next 12 months.

All it took was a little bit of confidence, the clarity that the conversation was to learn more about his career, and the faith that nothing wrong will come from asking for a 20-minute meeting. This, Mi Gente, is what I challenge you to do when you want to network within your own company.

YOU PICK, I PAY

Here is another internal networking tip I want to share with you that helps remove the awkwardness of asking for a meeting. I call this "You Pick, I Pay." I use this idea only when I have met someone before but I do not know them very well and I want to get to know them better. It can be a little forward to just email someone internally and say, "Hey, can we talk?" So to make the conversation flow easier, I invite people to lunch by saying, "You Pick, I Pay." This small play on words helps open doors, mainly because everyone has to eat and it's a friendly way to invite someone to connect.

My best example of how I have used this effectively is when I wanted to get to know my employer's Chief General Counsel better. The man was young, extremely intelligent, and had a PhD. His story was intriguing to me because why would an attorney get a PhD and how did he become Chief General Counsel before he was 45 years old? While we might have seen each other in the hallway, we did not know each other beyond first names.

He had a corner office, I did not. He had a secretary, I did not. He was part of our executive leadership, I was not. But I did not allow his rank, title or company stature keep me from asking him to share his story. So I sent an email. I wrote, *"I read your biography on the company website and I am impressed by your pedigree. It's not often that I meet an attorney who also has a PhD. Currently, I am evaluating whether or not a PhD makes sense for my career and if your schedule permits, I would like to invite you to lunch to learn more about your career path. You pick the place and I will pay. I look forward to your response."*

Not only did the Chief General Counsel accept my invitation, since that first lunch session, we have had over 20 more lunch meetings. As our relationship developed, he would provide me insight on why the executive leadership team at our company made certain decisions, and I would use that information to navigate my own career. That "You Pick, I Pay" technique not only help me gain an advisor, I also gained a friend.

While not everyone may be receptive to your invitation for lunch, counter the objection with "would you like to go for a walk, take a coffee break at Starbucks, or just meet up for 10 minutes?" All you want to do is connect and get to know people on a deeper level. Whether you are networking internally or externally, the entire approach is about establishing a relationship and sharing your story.

Preparing Your Elevator Pitch

The best way to share your story and is by practicing your elevator pitch. When you think about your story, you must think in two dimensions, short- and long-term career goals. Short-term means the job you would like to have tomorrow. Long-term means the job you would like to have 10 years from now. Depending on the setting, including both goals may not be appropriate for your elevator pitch, but you should be prepared to provide a clear answer if you get asked to engage in the conversation further.

An elevator pitch is a 30-second blurb about you. The approach is simple, crafting the words can be a challenge, but I will share with you actual examples when I coached individuals on their pitch and will provide the before and after to give you an idea on how to sharpen yours. Here is the template I follow on how to create an elevator pitch:

1) Give Your Name
2) Share what problem you solve
3) Tell them why you decided to attend the networking event
4) Ask, "How Can I Help You?"

Real World Example #1:

Pitch before template:

- My name is Charles and I am a copy editor, designer and I am a problem solver. I want to work with publications to bring them to the next level.

While the above pitch is less than 30 seconds, it does not give enough information to the listener on what makes Charles unique or what Charles is looking to do. We needed to dig deeper and clarify what problems copy editors solve. Per Charles, copy editors look for accuracy in publications, grammar usage, and checking quality of facts. In essence, his job is to make things "pop on paper."

After Template:
After a handful of revisions and a few practice runs, this is Charles' new elevator pitch:

- My name is Charles and I am a copy editor and designer.
- I pride myself on making things pop on paper, by having my work be clear, legible and readable.

- I am here because I want to meet other people who share my same ambition
- Please let me know if there are problems I can solve for you to have your products reach your readers.

Real World Example #2

Pitch before template:

- My name is Jean, I have a wide array of experience and I want to help millennials tell their story.

After Template:

- Hello, My name is Jean and I am a storyteller
- I focus on helping millennials of color achieve professional success by teaching them how to develop and share their unique story
- I am here because I am excited to meet more millennials of color who aspire to accomplish big things
- So please let me know if there is anything I can do for you as you establish your career.

That last line is important because if you can, you do not want to network when you need it but rather network from a position of strength and be a connector so you can help others. In return, by showing that you are problem solver, you will make yourself memorable and strengthen your personal brand by being perceived as a great person to know.

Successful elevator pitches come with practice. You cannot just write a pitch and believe you are done, you have to force yourself to be in an environment where you will articulate your story, see people's reaction, and modify it if you need to improve your pitch.

Not all People are Created Equal

I am certain that you have met people in your life who are gifted in different areas. You may have a friend who is strong academically, while you may have an equally important friend who is gifted with athletic ability. At the end of the day, we are not all created equal. There are certain people who will be better than you from just natural ability. That only means that you need to invest the time and slay away at the vision you have set out for yourself. Invest the necessary hours to elevate your personal development. Make the time to learn about your industry, the industry you want to break into, and the current trends that are affecting you and your future employer. You must be unapologetic with your commitment to excel. As Latinos, we multi-task so much that we hardly have time to focus on one thing. Put the time into yourself. Selling yourself requires self-awareness, confidence, and the commitment to just *try*. Feeling good about your elevator pitch is your beginning. Practice it and own it!

From Pan Dulce to Bagels w/ Cream Cheese: The Art of Cultural Code Switching

Sweet Bread! Who amongst us did not grow up with sweet bread? Watching our parents dip pan dulce into a cup of coffee was as normal as watching the sun shine through a window.

Pan dulce was such a common staple in my household that I did not value its worth until the day came that I lived in a neighborhood where pan dulce was no longer easy to find and I was being offered bagels with cream cheese instead. I experienced it and you might, too – a level of insecurity and awkwardness when you are removed from your comfort zone.

Whether it's a trust factor, where you may not yet feel comfortable opening up with your colleagues or you feel that your colleagues do not value your input, it is your responsibility to make the best of the situation and figure it out. With that said, I have felt this way in many situations, and the feeling gets compounded when you are the only Latino in the office, because there is no one else there that can relate to you. To preserve your own sanity, you must hit the switch and put on your game face.

While I learned how to appreciate bagels with cream cheese, I learned how to live in a world that was quickly becoming my new normal. Pan dulce is my metaphor that connects me to my most simple and basic Latino customs, but bagels with cream cheese also serves as my symbol that personifies a piece of my life in Corporate America. Both are good, but neither has anything to do with each other, for the exception that I consume both. Today, both represent me, but in order for me to balance both worlds (home and corporate life), I had to learn the art of cultural code switching.

To gain additional perspective on the topic of cultural code switching, I interviewed several individuals to learn how they managed the cultural transition from home to corporate. I wanted to know how they learned to be good at cultural code switching as they began building their personal brands at work, and if the cultural switching caused them any problems in the workplace.

I want to share with you the personal stories of two Latino leaders, Valentina and Marco, who mastered the art of cultural code switching in their own special way and have carved out impressive careers because of their keen ability to leverage their homegrown skills and transfer them into their corporate environment.

First, I want you to meet Valentina. Valentina is a Mexican-American woman from California who graduated from an elite all-woman's college on the East Coast and is currently a Director at a Fortunate 100 company.

Valentina's Story
I am a Mexican woman, born in California and my parents were farm workers. Scholarship money was important to me because my parents were not in a position

to financially contribute to my education in any capacity. So when it was time for me to apply to college, I focused on schools where the financial expense would not burden my parents and that sole desire forced me to mainly focus on state schools.

For the exception of applying to only one school on the East Coast who were known to give healthy financial aid packages, I was resigned to staying in California. When I was admitted to college on the East Coast, I jumped at the chance to enroll immediately because I knew that my life's trajectory was about to change for the better. I am Latina, female, Southern-California girl who loved school but the punishing winters on the East Coast were something I was not ready to experience. Living on the East Coast was different too, because Mexicans were not the overwhelming majority as we are in California. I liked it though, because I gained great friendships with people from other parts of Latin America and also developed strong bonds with people who were not Latino at all.

When I graduated from college, I decided to move back to California to be close to family. I secured a job working in the non-profit sector, specifically for a microloan fund where we focused on helping small business reestablish themselves and rebuild their credit. The work was important to me, because at the time, my hometown was hurting. It was soon after the Rodney King riots and many small businesses needed assistance to jump-start their businesses again. This experience opened my eyes to the importance I can contribute to my community and I wanted to do more on a larger scale.

After searching for various opportunities, I decided to join a Latino-focused legal defense fund that made big impacts on the national stage. Working for such a well-renowned organization exposed me to the struggles that Latinos face nationality. I was well aware of the struggles of farm workers, as I myself lived that experience. I was also well aware of the struggles that Latinos faced on the east coast, but to serve in the capacity of management at the defense fund further sharpened my ability to not only think strategically on how to tackle varying issues, but to also learned when and how to collaborate with other organizations to address issues that impact multiple communities. My love for my culture positioned me to pursue a career that was meaningful. However, I felt that I had to impact change on a larger scale and decided to leave the non-profit arena and change careers to pursue an opportunity at a Fortune 100 company.

My drive for this change was personal. Many Latinos are in non-profit, but more need to be in Corporate America. I see the good work that corporations aim to do in the community, and I wanted to be a voice in that arena. I also wanted to be a force to change the corporate culture from the inside, by playing within the rules, and creating pipelines, pathways and roadmaps for other Latinos to also gain the courage to apply to work for large companies. Now that we are on the inside, we must open the door for the rising generation. We are representing a community of people and we want to make our families and communities proud of our achievements. So I decided to go big!

For me, finding my niche in Corporate America was easier than what I initially anticipated. As a Latina, I was raised to be upbeat, say hello, introduce myself, build relationships, be committed, work hard and be loyal. Those simple attributes are transferrable skills to a corporate environment. Those skills lay the foundation for a career in business development, marketing, sales operations, and more. Furthermore, as Latinos, we tend to be risk takers. While we will calculate the risk, we tend to move quickly and that is something not everyone can do. I believe we can use this to our advantage because we possess eager spirits to make things happen, and that attitude is highly valued and appreciated. While these may be the soft skills to business, they are not always prevalent with other colleagues and as such, place us on a different path to get noticed.

As a child, I would translate for my mother. As I grew older, I would continue to translate for my mother and I developed a keen skill to think in two languages, be fluent in two languages, and I stepped right up when my company asked me if I would participate in meeting with dignitaries from Latin America who were interested in learning how our services could help serve their country. I was not shy or insecure with my abilities. I used my bilingual ability to get ahead at work because I was one of the few employees who could relate to our clients, and position our company as a resource to a growing customer population both here in the U.S. and abroad. Through this experience, and leveraging my skills, I learned that I could have meetings with diplomats from Latin American countries the same way I can have meetings with CEO's in this country.

Now, working in Corporate America is different. There is a certain understanding that must be learned in order to do well here. As with any facet of life, there is a game that must be played. Working hard is a given. You are expected to work hard. Meeting budgets and deadlines is a given. You are expected to come under budget and produce great work in the time allotted. I was raised to be humble, not to rock the boat, and to be grateful to have a job. Unfortunately, that Latino/immigrant mentality does not always work in Corporate America. You must have confidence, and as Latinos, we must learn how to balance our humility and our ability to be leaders. Leadership does not come with titles. Convey the executive presence. Show that you can inspire confidence in other people too. Work on developing your executive presence, and master your ability to connect the dots when faced with problems and brainstorming solutions. Make yourself valuable by showing how you helped the company see things that they did not see without your perspective. More importantly, learn to convey your message in tangible terms, meaning, for instance, that you earned the company money by decreasing inefficiencies, reduced waste, improved customer satisfaction scores and by gaining a competitive advantage over a competitor.

My biggest strength is my executive presence. With heels on, I am a whopping 5'2" tall, but I walk and talk like I am 6'1". Bring your confidence, and your ability to instill confidence in others into the work environment. Be willing to work with people, seek out people who think differently and know things that are different from you. Surround yourself with people who are different from you, folks who challenge your thinking. Don't get defensive, but rather, embrace what you can learn.

As a Latino, you must possess the confidence that you can be a business leader, community leader, play a game of loteria on Sunday night and break down a business case on Monday morning. With that said, have the smarts to build alliances. Learn how to pick your battles. I make it a point to come extremely prepared to meetings, I ask for help when I do not know something, and I make the time to meet people from other departments so they can better understand what I do and so I can learn what they do. This, my friends, is called networking within your own tribe. I work for a large multinational company. I do not know everyone, but I make it a point to get to know the people who I believe I need to know. I am constantly finding mentors and champions to both help me think problems through and advocate for my professional development when I am being considered for a new role. When possible, I go outside my comfort zone because I want my bosses to know that I am comfortable with ambiguity. As a Latina farm worker whose family lived with uncertainty, thriving in ambiguity is what I know. There will be a time when you fail and that will be okay. People are not interested to see if you fall, but rather to watch to see how you get back up, so don't be afraid to fall.

Lastly, I want to share the importance of being involved. Be active in corporate volunteer opportunities. Raise your hand to serve on extracurricular activities, and if your company has a Latino employee resource group, become active. While the role of an ERG may vary from company to company, do not negate the fact that they serve a role. The role is to enhance the Latino employee work experience. As with anything, you get what you invest and, similar to high school, the kids who do well are the ones who do extra-curricular activities.

The ERG helps develop exposure among the company and to network internally, but also remember the politics that are involved. You are an employee of the company first. As committed as we may be to change corporate culture or open the door for the next generation, we need to remember to be excellent in our roles because we are there to do a job. Also, the higher you go, the fewer Latinos there are, but the ERG is an effective tool for those who are able to network through it. There is power to mobilize as a community and be able to move forward.

As I interviewed Valentina, I loved how she spoke about the balance of excelling at work but also changing the culture from within. I believe in that philosophy! As Latinos who aspire to achieve success in Corporate America, there is an element where we must play by the rules. Our success is predicated on the support of people who do not look like us or even understand our struggles, yet, transforming these folks to be our allies is critical to our success. It's all about the relationships, and sharing our pan dulce, embracing differences, and enjoying a serving of bagels with cream cheese is a great start to effectively building our relationships.

How to Compete When You Don't Know How

I am confident that during your career, you have heard the old adage, "You don't know what you don't know." That statement does not get any clearer than describing the experience on what to do when you have your first job and you are trying to figure out how to get ahead in your company. For many Latinos who have secured their first job in Corporate America, this is all too familiar. I want to introduce you to Marco. I interviewed Marco to gain his perspective on how Latinos rise, fall and must learn how to rise again in Corporate America when there is no one around to teach you how. Marco earned his bachelor's degree in marketing, worked for a consumer packaged goods company and now is a consultant for one of the most elite consulting firms in the country. Marco lives in New York City, and in his own words, here is his perspective on the need to be successful at cultural code switching.

Marco's Story

I want to start by telling you that I love both my mother and father. As most Latino parents, they sacrifice their entire being in order to help their children. They poured everything they had into me and while I felt their support and appreciated everything they did for me, when I was in college, I felt grossly underprepared to compete for top tier jobs. I do not blame them for anything because they did the best they could, but like most Latino parents, they were not able to give me advice on careers because they themselves were not exposed to the type of career I wanted to pursue. My parents did not have a network of professional friends to leverage to help me figure out what companies to research or opportunities to seek. As a first generation Latino, I was struggling to find my way. Not surprisingly, some of my classmates who did not share my background where scheduling informational interviews in New York City to meet with friends of family friends who worked at the major investment banking firms. Their reality was just different than mine. While I knew I had the book smarts to compete, I had not yet developed the social skills to be more competitive at higher levels. Through sheer grind, I secured an incredible opportunity in marketing for a consumer packaged goods company focused on cereal, canned goods, and yogurt. I secured this job through on-campus recruiting; otherwise, I would have not known how to get myself in front of a hiring manager.

My parents were proud of me and they did give me career advice when I started. My folks told me to work hard, stay humble, produce high quality work and trust that my managers will notice. On the surface, that was great advice and almost impossible to refute because who does not want to do well. I say impossible because I later experienced that trusting my managers to notice did not always work out in my best interest.

As a Latino in Corporate America, there is a balancing act of living in two different worlds. Understanding the term bi-cultural requires you to acknowledge that there is the business culture and the family culture. Where Latinos fall short is in the skill of selling ourselves. The culture in business is about "I," as in 'The contributions that I made to the team lead to a higher than expected return on investment.' Whereas at home, our custom is about the "We," as in 'The contributions that we did together allowed us to achieve a higher than expected return on investment.' While the difference may be subtle, in Latino households if we put ourselves above anyone else, that action is not only just highly frowned upon but also makes you seem like someone who is "muy creido"… arrogant. This awareness limits our career potential because in interviews, as Latinos we do not frame our answers to focus on the contributions we made individually. We need to learn how to celebrate our individual achievements more because that's how career advancement is awarded. I also feel that the learning curve will be different for us because we do not fully know what we are walking into. If you don't come from a prep school or have a family that knows, how do you prepare yourself to be competitive? Our parents are not in positions to teach us how to advocate for ourselves and as such, we are left to figure it out as we go.

After an almost 10-year career in marketing, I decided to leave my employer to pursue an MBA degree full-time. I was proud that I was admitted to an ivy-league business school program ranked in the Top 10 in the world. However, even with that crowning achievement, once I got to business school my eyes were wide open to learn the dynamics of how business moves, and once again how little I knew about the inner working of networking. While in business school, I was *able to switch careers and I moved away from consumer goods to management consulting. I was thrilled for my new opportunity and because of my prior work experience I felt less awkward about being one of the few Latinos in my firm. I was focused and my mindset was set to excel. I learned that I cannot be competitive in a world that is not aligned with my beliefs and because of that, I forced myself to learn how to network both internally and externally so I would not have an uneasy feeling. I made the effort to meet people and even began developing relationships with senior managers and a few partners. Out of the class that joined the consulting group with me, I could visibly see that I was making the hardest effort to cultivate relationships within the firm as compared to my peer colleagues. I felt good about my proactive approach to building allies, until I realized my approach on how to build such relationships was incomplete.*

When it came time to our annual review, I felt I was shortchanged. However, one of my colleagues who started with the company at the same time as I did and who relied on me to help her decipher various problems with a client's engagement actually earned a higher rating on her review than I received on mine. As a matter of fact, she was heralded as the highest-ranking first-year associate. I was floored! This woman relied on me for help and I was told I needed more improvement in a handful of areas.

What I experienced was eye-opening. In essence, white people have the courage to 'go for it' and will schedule time with high-ranking leaders to get informal performance feedback well before evaluations begin. My colleague was a savvy individual who scheduled meetings with our boss's boss to ask for performance feedback. I cannot hold anything against her because she simply outplayed me, and taught me a valuable lesson about making allies with company leaders who sit at high levels. For her, achieving the best score, highest rating was an expectation, right, entitlement, and her confidence was rooted in privilege. By no means was she nasty, but culturally speaking, she had the heart to go for it all the way and I was more reserved, almost hoping that my manager would see that I was contributing to my team's success at a greater level that the rest of my teammates. I followed the advice my parents gave me to work hard and my boss will notice. Unfortunately, that was not the case and again, that falls on me.

As Latinos, we are more reserved than our white colleagues. We need to stop seeking communal approval that it's okay to move forward and aspire for more. My white friends do not bound their voice and Latinos don't speak up enough. We need to be more political, we need to understand the social cues of interviewing, the social cues of internal networking, we need to share our opinions more effectively, and lastly, we need to learn how to play the game better.

Marco's words resonated with me because the advice that Latino parents give their children is almost as if they practiced it in unison, "Work hard, and your manager will notice." Marco's experience may have elements that may resonate with you, especially the part that *"we do not go for it enough."* I had many takeaways from Marco's interview, ranging from loving our parents, not being well prepared, and having a more reserved approach to business, but my biggest take away is when he expressed the importance of understanding the social cues of interviewing. There is a special way to interview with a greater focus on personal contributions versus team accomplishments. Celebrating yourself is important and when done with class and balance, it shows that you are a competitive candidate.

Recognizing the Social Cues of Interviewing

Based on Marco's story about understanding how to better understand the social cues of interviewing, I want to focus on how to prepare for an interview if you are applying to business school. I want to reiterate my belief that one of the best ways to achieve success in Corporate America is by earning your Master of Business Administration degree. This degree will position you to compete for higher paying jobs and will also help you further your career as you become more competitive and refine your business savviness.

Effective interviewing requires skill. While a good interview does not guarantee that you will move forward in the process, a bad interview does guarantee that you will stop moving at all. Therefore, learning effective interviewing requires practice. Your job is to invest the time to become effective at interviewing.

All interviews create the same jitters. Whether you are interviewing for the first time in your professional life, or you are a seasoned professional seeking your next challenge in life, there is a nervous energy that must be channeled, prep-time that must be invested, and above all, you must know how to tell your story. If you are interviewing for a job, or interviewing at your No.1 business school, there are similarities. You will get asked standard questions, such as:

Three Common MBA Interview Questions:

- Walk me through your resume.
- What are your short-term and long-term goals?
- What are your strengths and weaknesses?

While these three real world questions are often asked, there are subtle differences that lie within the social cues from the interviewer that determine if these interviews have successful outcomes or fall short of gaining business school admission. Recognizing that social cues in interviewing are absolutely real, social cues are only occasionally discussed and seldom practiced on how to identify them while you are actually being interviewed.

To be on the same page, let's define social cues. Simply stated, social cues are the verbal or nonverbal, positive or negative signals that people send through body language. While the cues can range from facial expressions and hand gestures to vocal tone, to those who are new at interviewing, it is not uncommon to miss the cues if the interview is slowly taking a wrong turn. For many applying to business school, your career may still be developing and you might not have had many (more than 10) formal interviews with various corporations to build a solid foundation on what to look for from interviewers.

All interviews begin the moment you walk into the building where the interview will be conducted. At that point, all eyes are on you. It has been documented that a first impression will be made within the first 19 seconds of meeting you! The moment someone says "Hello" to you … it's game on. The way you respond is your cue on how your first impression will be received.

The Art of Small Talk

An interview is the evaluation of your soft and hard skills. However, decisions are based on a relationship. As the interviewee, it is your responsibility to establish a rapport with the interviewer. Small talk is important. When your interview begins and you are asked, "How was your commute in? Did you find parking easy enough? How are you doing?" Your response must be positive, upbeat, and complimentary to them for making it easy for you to meet with the interviewer; and one-word answers such as, "Good, Yes, and Fine" are unacceptable.

Your ability to make small talk will set the tone and create a positive impression that you are a confident individual. More importantly, the enthusiastic smile on your face, your high energy, and your thorough answers will be the success factors that will dictate your ability to move forward in the interview process.

The Art of the Response

You can answer any question in multiple ways. However, you need to find one way that is genuine to you in order to have a great answer. As a suggestion, here are a few sample responses to the questions above for you to consider as you practice your answers:

- "My commute was great. I knew rush hour traffic would be a challenge, so I gave myself an extra 30 minutes to get here and it worked out well. I actually enjoyed my commute today."

- "Parking was extremely easy. I have heard that parking downtown can be a challenge, but I gave myself plenty of time to get here and I found parking without any problems."
- "My day is going great. I am excited to meet you and I have been looking forward to our conversation this entire week."

Your enthusiasm will set the tone and perhaps even put the interviewer in a more relaxed, friendly mood, as they will appreciate your positive persona. However, in case you get an interviewer who seems to be more scripted in how they ask you questions, be conscious of their body language as the interview progresses.

READING BODY LANGUAGE

A common frustration with interviews is when the interviewee is not able to properly read the interviewer's reaction to your questions. As much as interviewing is a skill, being an interviewer is also a skill and not every person who interviews prospective candidates is a capable interviewer. With that said, you must recognize that they are a gatekeeper and you are responsible to find some common ground. For example, be aware of their eye contact. If your interviewer is glancing around the room, it's a signal that your responses may be long. Do not be perceived as a rambler. Be concise and prepared to shorten your answers if you see that the interviewer's attention to your words is drifting.

Vocal tone is an important factor to the successful flow of interviews. If the interviewer begins to say, *"Ah, Okay, I see,"* while you are still responding to their question, that is your cue to shorten your response and stop. Be mindful of how they react to your answers. Ultimately, you want to have a positive experience. You want to leave the interview feeling proud. Practice interviewing. Practice responding with succinct answers. Invest the time to become effective and have the courage to interview as much as you can.

Once again, remember that while a good interview does not always move you forward, a bad interview will always keep you back. Your first impression is critical, so maintain a positive demeanor. Recognizing the social cues of MBA interviewing is a skill and with the right coaching, this is a skill that you can master!

Don't Rock The Boat

As we read in the prior chapter, cultural code switching can be a challenge. Our parents tell us to be humble, work hard, and to be loyal. We are told to, in not so many words, to not rock the boat. My parents saw America as a huge opportunity for me – and one that they worked hard for. For many Latinos who come here, there is an idea that being here is opportunity enough. My parents had immeasurable gratitude for living in a place that would allow me a better life. So did I, but I also wanted more.

Often, as Latinos we are told not to "rock the boat" – not to take what we have for granted. From a cultural standpoint, I understand it, but what parents don't realize is that in telling their kids not to question or push for change, they aren't positioning them to be leaders. Kids can be torn between their parents' view and their own desire for more.

The best example I have to illustrate this point was when I told my father that I was seeking a career change. At the age of 33, I had achieved some of my professional and personal goals, but I wanted to stretch further. I wanted to achieve more. After graduating with my MBA at the age of 28, I was recruited to work for General Motors. My career was great, but I hit a plateau in my career at GM and felt that it was time to move on. I had received an offer to join Volkswagen, the maker of the Beetle – the exact car my father sold to come to America, and I told my father that I was going to leave. My father was disappointed with my decision. In his eyes, here was this amazing job with a multi-national corporation that I was able to break into and now I wanted to leave. He told me that they had been so good to me, and wanted to know why I would ever dream of leaving.

My father stressed that I had to be loyal. I believe in loyalty, but there is a balance between loyalty and opportunity. While frustrated, I could not be angry with my dad. He just did not understand the culture of Corporate America. The question at hand was not whether or not I should remain loyal, but rather, can I continue to grow at GM. I decided to leave because I could grow faster at VW. While saddened with my decision, my father simply did not understand that changing companies is part of the process of professional growth. More importantly, it has also been documented that staying with one company can actually put you at a long-term disadvantage, when it comes to negotiating salary, position, title and upward mobility in your career path. I had to rock the boat, and quickly shed the guilt that loyalty was superior to personal fulfillment.

Comfort can come with a cost, but for us Latinos, we often have to hear how we should be grateful for what we have. Wanting more is a good thing – especially if you want to set yourself apart as a leader. It is important to look at what your goals are and what you need to achieve them, even if that means doing something like changing companies, jobs, or even industries. Change forces us to grow and learn new things, which makes us better at what we set out to do.

CHAPTER 4

Latino History through Personal Stories

• • •

As I think through the number of challenges that Latinos in America have to overcome to achieve a level of success, I feel compelled to also talk about our Latino history and the stories we share from our past. As I thought about what Latino history meant, our people and culture is so rich and vast that there is no one history that can encompass who we are as people, but rather, our history is expressed through numerous stories. Latinos come from Europe, Africa, the Caribbean, Central and South America. Each has a rich history and a story all its own.

However, it is my opinion that the most important history, is your personal story. Where did your family and relatives come from? What traditions and cultures did they bring with them? How much of that rich history was lost when they came to America? In essence, what's your story and how can you leverage your story to achieve success?

Personally, my story is based on dreamers, which means my family came here with a dream of what I would do with my life in America. They did not come here with the idea of just having a better life for themselves. My father worked hard labor his whole life. Hard labor is hard labor, no matter where you are in the world.

We each have a story, our own personal history of how we got here, what our parents sacrificed for us, and what we did for the gift they gave us, the freedom to choose the life we want. I have met so many Latino brothers and sisters who do not take advantage of the gift given to them. Some are afraid. Others don't know how. Worse still are those who do not believe they should aspire for big things because they were raised to focus on a task – mostly work – and to not think of grandeur.

Because I firmly believe that our history is about the sharing of stories, I went on a mission to find other Latinos and I interviewed them so I could share their stories. I spent hours upon hours speaking with other people who looked like us, had challenges similar to us and are working to overcome the various challenges they face. The premise of my book is to inspire and teach other Latinos how to rise above the hardships we have endured, but sometimes it's helpful to hear the message from a different voice. As I share each individual's story, I am sharing their story through their voice. The same way they told me. I want to capture the passion, authenticity, and pure essence of their words. We all have a beginning. Many start with bigger obstacles, but most do *Rise Up* once they commit themselves to finding a roadmap to achieve success. I will step back now and let them speak.

I want to honor a man who has dedicated his life to be a school teacher and help Latino youth find purpose. When we look for male role models, Mario fits the bill. He is a man whose vision, motivation and commitment to help Latino youth achieve greatness are inspiring. I appreciate his honesty, his struggles, and his desire to help. His story of coming to America is the story that we hear in passing, but many of the details are typically left out. Mario goes into detail and shares his fears, his hopes, and how he used his opportunity to become a professional in America. As Latinos, we all take different paths to get here. I believe in the power of roadmaps. There will never be one single path to achieve a goal, but all you need to do is follow one path to achieve your goals. Mario had his roadmap and here is his story!

Mario's Story
My name is Mario, and I was born in Venezuela. My father was a shoemaker, and my grandfather was a shoemaker. My entire family were shoemakers. I

usually tell people who if we didn't have the opportunity to come to this country, I probably would have been a shoemaker because there were no other opportunities where we lived. We were an extremely poor family of five. It was my father and my mother and the three of us children.

We used to live in a room that was one-third the size of my classroom today at the high school where I teach in Chicago. All of us in that one room. Some days my father would get up and go and he would tell my mother, "I am going to try look for work but I'm coming back."

And we would wait without any food, no breakfast, just waiting for my father to go out there and hustle and try to find some money or a job for the day. We would watch the door waiting from him to come home. He would return home late, sometimes with ten pesos, or twenty pesos. If we were lucky, it might be a dollar, two dollars, or five dollars and he tell my mother, "Do whatever you can."

My mother would go out and buy milk and bread or potatoes and get creative and do whatever she could for that day. The next day he went back out and did the same thing.

My mom and dad shared our one bed. My sister had the bottom of the bed and my brother and I slept on the floor. I never had a refrigerator at home until we came to this country, and never had telephone. We never had the common things people have today until we came to the U.S.

My uncle was the first person who migrated to the states in 1967 but then he returned in 1979 to Venezuela to get his green card. My uncle lived in Chicago and that was his adopted home. He visited us and saw how poor and desperate we were and he told my father, "I want to help you out. You're my brother, and I love you. I want to help you, but you have a large family. You have five people. I can't afford to bring five people. So why don't I help you and the boys."

At the time I was 14 and my brother was 15. "I'll help you and the boys to come to the states. When you guys get there, you work hard and you send for the rest of the family."

We agreed with the plan. We wanted to come to the U.S. legally and we applied for a visa. We went to the U.S. Embassy to apply, but in order to be given a visa you have to show that you have a reason to come back, that you have a *financial attachment to the country, and you're not just going to stay in the US. You had to have a plan to return to Venezuela.*

Somehow my father was able to get all these fake documents such as income tax returns and bank statements that showed that he had some money. At least that's what the papers said, but when you looked at our faces it was evident, it was so clear that we were poor and that those papers were fake.

We went to the Embassy and were denied a visa. So we moved to Plan B, which was to go through Mexico. At that time, you could get a visa to Mexico just by showing that you had tickets and you were going there as a tourist. We left Venezuela in 1980 and arrived in Mexico City. We met my uncle there. He had flown from New York to meet us. We spent two days in Mexico getting everything ready. My cousin and her 4-year-old daughter were also coming with us.

My uncle had made arrangements and had hired a person who was going to get us across the border, and would receive payment once we were safely delivered to where my uncle was waiting for us in San Diego. My uncle instructed the individual that was going to get us across to not spare any expenses, and to make sure we were comfortable. My father was given instructions on what to do when we got to the airport in Tijuana. "They're going to ask you why you're there," our escort told us, "Tell them you're there as a tourist. They're not going to believe you. They're going to charge you a fee."

They told my father to have money ready and to give them $200, which was per $50 per person. Back then, they would take the bribe and let you go.

When we arrived at the airport the Mexican police made us line up, Mexicans on one side and foreigners on the other. They asked us, "Where are you coming from?"

"Venezuela," we said.

"Why are you here?"

"As tourists," we replied.

They laughed and said, "Who are you kidding? There's nothing to do here. There's a desert in this direction and a desert in that direction. You're either here to bring drugs or to cross the border. So which is it?"

At 14, I remember being searched at the airport in places that I had never been searched in my life. They told me, "Pull your pants down." They searched us, making sure that we were not bringing in drugs.

When they were done we paid the fee to the Mexican police, and they let us go. They had told us specifically that once we got out of the airport, for us not to get in a yellow taxi. Take one of the white vans or white taxis. I don't know why, but that is what they told us.

We got to the gate and they wouldn't let us go across to where the white taxis were. So we had no choice but to get into this yellow taxi. And the taxi driver starts asking, "Where are you guys from? Where are you visiting from?"

"Venezuela."

"Okay." Then he starts playing with his rear view mirror, like giving signals to someone. We get pulled over by the Mexican police again. They get us out the car, they tell us, "You're here to cross the border."

And that's when we were kidnapped by the Mexican police for about a day and a half. They told us, "You're here to cross the border. We're going to let you cross the border, but you're going to cross the border with the person that we give you. You can't just cross the border with anyone. We're going to take you to someone, that person is going to get you across the border. Do you have relatives waiting?"

"Yes, we have relatives in the US. They're going to pay." We were desperate. They took us, and we were driving around for hours and finally they took us to someone up in the hills where there was a small house. They had us locked up in that house with the new people who were going to get us across. It was a family, a husband, a wife and a kid. And the police gave us to them.

My cousin kept on talking and talking and talking to the wife and said, "Look, you're a mother. I'm a mother. We're not going anywhere. We already agreed that you're going to get us across the border. My family in the U.S. is going to pay you. All I want to know is when are you going to get us across the border?"

"Tomorrow. Tomorrow."

My cousin said, "Look, just take us to a hotel where we can stay the night. I just want to shower. I want to give my daughter a shower. We want to rest so that we'll be ready for tomorrow."

My cousin tried to work from a mother-to mother-approach. The lady convinced the husband, "Why don't we take them to a motel, let them stay there." They did leave us at a motel but the police were guarding the entrance of the parking lot so that we would not escape. We were able to make a phone call to the people who my uncle had arranged for us to go with across the border. They came at three in the morning, put us in the trunk of a car and took us out of that motel. We drove right past the police that were guarding that entrance and we escaped!

The next day, we crossed the border in Tijuana. When we arrived at the Mexican side of the border, there were thousands of people selling stuff like clothes, burritos, and various other items. It's like a flea market and everyone is trying to get you to buy stuff before you cross.

When it gets dark it's like a procession. Hundreds of people just start walking to try to get across. It's amazing; people think that it's just a group of two or three people trying to get across. No, it's hundreds of people.

So we started walking, and we had our two guides with us. Remember you are in the middle of a desert. You walk all night and the next day we rested all day. There was a house made of tires, like a cave, and there are gallons of water for you to drink while you waited for the sun to go back down again. You don't move during the day because you're easily spotted. So you rest all day and then you walk all night. We did that for two days.

We were near U.S. territory and we were picked up by a car – a little Toyota Corolla. Since there were five of us, they put three of us in the trunk, and two people in the backseat. We drove and drove and drove. At one point the driver stopped and said, "I got to be honest with you. This is my first journey. This is the first time I am making this trip and I am lost. I'm lost. I don't know where we are."

My cousin went to the nearest door, knocked, and asked the people inside to let her borrow a phone. She called and got directions, but we had to stay another day in the middle of nowhere. We couldn't get across because immigration was out there, so we waited another day.

Fortune smiled, and it was Labor Day, a federal holiday. We were able to get across the border, because many of the border patrol officers had the day off. We met up with a pickup truck which they loaded with tires and covered, to make it look like they were hiding people in there. We followed in the Corolla with all of us in the trunk.

The plan was if immigration or police spot us, the pickup truck will take off and they'll think that's the one with the people. They were a decoy.

We drove that way for two hours.

Finally, we pull over and the guy who was the leader gets out of the car and says, "What the hell are you guys still doing in the trunk? What are you doing hiding back there? We went across the border like an hour ago." He was just laughing and laughing.

My brother and I got in the back of the pickup truck. No cover. I just remember driving and being on the highway and it seeing signs that said Los Angeles and San Diego and we knew that we had arrived. When we arrived at a house in San Diego where my uncle was waiting for us at a house, we were relieved. We all quickly took showers and then we were off to L.A.

In L.A., we spent about three days looking around the city and then we took a flight out to Chicago O'Hare Airport. At that time, we did not need any ID to board the plane. We had passports when we left Venezuela but they were taken from us in Tijuana, so we just boarded with our tickets, no questions asked. We arrived in Chicago where my uncle lived and we began a new chapter of our lives. It was the beginning of the school year, and so it was decided my brother and I would go to school. My uncle went with us looking for schools. A couple of the schools in the area didn't have an ESL, bilingual program, so they kept on sending us from one place to another. In 1980, ESL programs were not mandatory like they are today. We did eventually find a school to attend.

We were lucky to arrive when we did in the U.S. This was during the Reagan administration, and he gave amnesty for millions of undocumented immigrants to become legal. The fact that we came in through Mexico was a good thing because there was no record of us entering in the airport. I really owe it to my uncle, who became like a second father to me. He was able to get creative and find papers that we had attended middle school, whenever we had to show that we had been here. He also got a letter from the priest saying that we had been attending their church for a couple of years. He did whatever he needed to show proof that we had been here so that we could look legitimate. My uncle submitted our papers to get our *work permits and our green card, but that was three years after we came to the U.S. I remember going for jobs and we used to buy blank or fake SSN and just put any number and then use it while looking for a job.*

I had a Spanish teacher, who was not a native Spanish speaker, tell my brother and I that we weren't allowed to enter his classroom the next day unless we showed him our green card. We went home and we told my uncle, the teacher says we can't go to class unless we show our green card. My uncle didn't say anything.

The next morning, we were ready for school, and my Uncle came with us to speak with the principal. My uncle explained that it was illegal to ask a student for a green card. I always remember that. Even in his limited English he knew what was legal and he made the principal understand that although he didn't know much English, he knew what the law says and this was illegal. We were allowed back in the class.

It was a tough high school we attended. We had a group of about nine Latinos, comprised of cousins and close friends. Unfortunately, out of our group, I was the only one that was able to finish high school and walk away with a high school diploma. It took my five years because I wouldn't speak English. I don't think that was an excuse, it was that I was rebellious. I started cutting class and I dropped out for about a year. Then I met a young lady who was a good influence in my life. She gave me an ultimatum – I could see her as long as I went to school.

"If you want to continue to see me, you got to go inside the school. If you really want to see me, you got to go to class. If you want to continue to see me, you got to pass your classes," she told me.

That got me back in school and back on the right track. She just kept on telling me I was very smart. She encouraged me to graduate and consider going to college. She actually filled out my college application for me.

My uncle went to our parent-teacher conferences whenever there was something in school. But when I started hanging out and cutting class, drinking, and doing things we weren't supposed to be doing, his support stopped. The school called him in and they told him what we were up to, "Your kid doesn't come to school, and he is not passing."

"I have my own two kids," he said, "and I've been to too many meetings. I never had to go to my own kid's meetings to be embarrassed, so I'm not coming back. I'm not coming back to school for you guys. So you're on your own."

I can understand and respect his decision. I knew other kids that came to the U.S. with or without their parents about my age. They are told, "You got to go to work. We got to pay back that money that we spent in bringing you here."

My uncle always said to me, "The only way you're going to repay me is by going to school and doing something positive with your life. That's the only payback that I want. Go to school and do something."

My father is a good man, he was working all day as a shoemaker and didn't have the time to go to school and do those kinds of parenting activities. I don't think my father ever went to our school when we were in high school, because he was working all the time. When I graduated from high school I told him, "Dad, I finished. I graduated." He replies, "Oh, I thought you had dropped out about a year ago." That is how in tune he was, but I don't hold it against him because he was focused on working hard and he was able to bring the rest of our family to join us in the U.S.

My father did tell me, "You got to go to school. You got to do something. You got to be better than I am. I don't want you fixing shoes. I don't want you polishing shoes. You got to go to school." Those words were always in the back of my mind.

I was surprised when I was actually accepted to college. I knew that I had a passion to help kids, but I also wanted to be involved with soccer. I decided to become a social studies teacher because I felt that by being a teacher I could coach soccer and stay close to my biggest passion in life. I coached for over seven years.

Today, now that I am a high school teacher, I see myself in many of my Latino students. A few are experiencing what I experienced, and while times are challenging, I remind myself of the time when I decided to temporarily dropout of high school, and decided to come back. I keep my high school and college transcripts right on my desk, right in front of me every day because it's a constant reminder that I can't give up on kids because I never know when they're going to turn it around. I did and so can they.

I look at my high school transcript and it shows a list of courses I failed. I failed 12 classes and so on the transcript it says, "Too many to be listed." It also reflects how in 11^(th) grade I dropped out of school. Then it shows how I finished school and I graduated from high school with a 68.9 average, and 65 was passing.

I look at my college transcript and it shows that I graduated with a 3.4 GPA. I went to a college locally for my undergraduate degree and then I pursued my first master's in second language learning. I earned a certificate of advanced study, which is in between a master's and a doctorate in school administration education leadership.

When I walk my hallways, when I see my kids that are graduating, when I see kids that are coming back to our community as professionals, I see the success stories. I think that we need to continue to look at the success stories, because I know we have a lot of challenges, but not every story has a sad ending.

My life story is simple compared to the stories I hear from my students. There are many kids who have gone through a lot more difficult things than I had, faced more challenges and they have become doctors and lawyers and I've been able to see it unfold. I'm amazed at the number of success stories that we have.

Latinos in the U.S. do have a number of challenges. Consider second generation Latinos. Their parents were often poor immigrants and they never had much. They have to work hard, often from 6:00 a.m. until 10:00 p.m. because they want to give their children everything they didn't have.

I see my job as a blessing, and I believe it gives my life purpose. I have the opportunity to change people's lives. If I can turn a regular kid into a doctor, how many lives am I saving? I can help change his life, the life of his children, and the life of his children's children.

My father died a year ago. When I look at my life I always say I'm successful. Looking where I came from and what I've been able to accomplish, I realize that my success is really his success. From where we started to where we are now, I accomplished many milestones and I'm set for life. I don't have to worry about anything else. At that same age, my father arrived in this country with my brother and me, without speaking the language, without a job, without anything. He started from zero at the same age that I am right now.

My success is really his success. To be my age and to say I got to start from zero, takes courage. He had to say to himself that he had to come to America and make sacrifices, risk his life and the life of my children so that they'll have a future, takes courage. I really respect him so much for that. I believe I have realized his dream and did not squander the gift he gave me – a chance to succeed and have a better life.

Luis' Story

I want to share with you Luis' story. Luis is an Ivy League educated Latino from East Los Angeles. I was attracted to his story because his humble beginnings reflect the reality of the working-class Latino. His educational accomplishments were not consistent with what many thought a Latino from East Los Angeles could actually achieve. Luis excelled both academically and professionally and I want to share his story with you.

I was born in East Los Angeles, and my parents were both from Mexico. My mom was from Zacatecas, and my Dad is from Tepic. In 1970, my father moved to East L.A. to meet with family from the town where he was born. He drove over the border, because back then, it was much easier. He still came across in a trunk, like contraband, but the borders were much freer, and you did not hear the horror stories like you do today.

He lived in East L.A. for 10 years before he met my mother. During that time he worked as a laborer installing chain link fences, which during the '70s was a booming business.

At first he worked with some of his friends and was paid under the table, but eventually he got a regular gig with a furniture maker. My father met my mom through mutual friends he was working with. My mother was in town visiting and that is how they connected.

My Mom had a tourist visa. My father came from a poorer background, where my mom grew up in a more middle class family in Mexico. My mother came in legally, but stayed illegally and got married to my father. My parents stayed undocumented until I was about 8.

When my father arrived and began working he got a fake Social Security card, but this was common. My mother had one too even when she had her tourist visa. My dad finally got his green card through amnesty, because he was working for a company. My mother got hers years later with the help of an attorney.

Growing up, things like being undocumented was not something I really paid attention to. Today kids are more afraid and understand what it means, but back in '80s it was not something we feared.

I was born in 1983, and I have a twin brother. We were the family translators, especially when it came to any kind of paperwork or contracts. My parents relied on us to translate because they had no one else to depend on.

Academics were important to our family and my brother and I both graduated college. I went to Brown University for my undergrad, and then I moved back home about five or six years. Eventually I went to Yale for my MBA.

My brother went to law school at Penn State, and after he finished he came back to L.A. We are both fortunate to have great careers.

Some people wonder how I ended up at Brown, as a kid from East L.A. I had an eccentric but good U.S. History teacher who cared about his students and challenged us to think bigger. There were only ten of us in his class, so it was easy for his passion to become contagious. During school, we had a mandatory reading time of twenty minutes a day. In an effort to think bigger, I decided to read a book from the 1960s that focused on personal upliftment. In that book, there was a reference to Brown University. That mention of Brown in the book just spoke to me and I was attracted to the program,

I did well on my SAT scores and in return, many schools were interested in me. I was motivated to do well, and even though I had great, supportive parents, they could not help us much. Dad only made it through the third grade and Mom went through the ninth grade. They encouraged us and pushed us to study hard and prioritize school.

Once I finished my undergrad I came home and began working for the government in the Housing Department. I worked there for three years and I had a friend that suggested I go to Yale for my Master of Business Administration degree. My parents were happy that I had a good government job, but they were not pushing me to go to grad school. They really did not understand what grad school could do for me, but they did understand the good job I was at and the security that it brought.

My father paid off their house, and talked to me about staying at my job so we could team up to buy a bigger house for the family. I was glad to go off to grad school, not because I did not love my parents but the transition to be independent actually helped our relationship. Going to grad school rather than just moving out made the transition a lot easier for everyone because the family knew I had a bigger goal I wanted to accomplish.

Even though both of my parents are from Mexico, we have lost our ability to speak Spanish over time. I can still read and write a little Spanish, but that is what happens when you are an American-born Latino, in order to assimilate you lose some of your heritage, language and culture.

I now work for an agency that is part of HUD (Housing and Urban Development), called Ginnie Mae. I work on housing finance policies. I got the job through a fellowship from the Presidential Management Fellows program that I finished during the summer. I am proud of my accomplishments and I know my family is too, and even though I have lost some of my Spanish-speaking skills, I never forget the sacrifices my family made for my brother and I, and I never forget why they came here, which was for a better life and a better life for us.

Jocelyn's Story

I want you to meet Jocelyn, a fourth-generation Latina who does not speak Spanish. While there can be a debate on whether Latinos should be able to speak Spanish, I want to provide a personal story of the struggles that a Latina has to address because she is not fluent in Spanish. It does not minimize her pride, and she still deals with the struggles that everyone of us have to overcome.

I am a Latina but I really don't speak Spanish other than what I learned in college. My father's side of the family is Spanish, from Spain; his family came to America and settled in a little town called Alamosa in Colorado, which is predominantly populated by Hispanics and Native Americans. I am a fourth-generation American, because my grandparents, great grandparents and father were born in America.

I was born in Glendale, California, but I really call Pasadena my home, because that is where I grew up and have spent my whole life. In fact, I still live here now. My family comes from a rich tradition, but over the generations it has changed. We practice some traditions that are very close to us, it's just the way that we know life, but it's not necessary Spanish, and it's not necessarily American. My grandparents speak broken Spanish. My grandfather speaks Spanish well, but never pure.

Since my father's family had settled in a small community, they always married other people who were Spanish, but that stopped during my father's generation. My father and all of his siblings married people who were not Spanish.

My mother's side is of German descent, but I still look enough like my father's side that other Hispanics identify me as one of their own. They often just start talking Spanish to me. Because I have a very light complexion, I'm curvy, and have curly hair, dark hair, people will ask – What are you? Are you mixed? Is there black in you? I get all sorts of questions.

Part of the reason for this is that there are a number of Moors who live in Spain, and many of the people in my family have a dark complexion, so I am a definitely an amalgamation of both sides. There are people in my father's family that have light colored eyes along with the darker skin. Some may look at them and say they look like Armenian or Jewish. Even though my family's roots are from Spain, and are Hispanic, they do not look as how people would envision Hispanics to look like, which for me is silly because our culture truly comes in many shapes and shades.

My husband has a dark complexion. He is third generation American and his family is from Mexico. He looks like someone from Mexico or South America, and like me, he does not speak Spanish. Other Hispanics become irritated because he does not speak his native tongue, even though for him and his family, America is where they were born and raised, where the expectation is that they speak English.

I am a mental health counselor, and there is this expectation that because I have a Hispanic background that I am expected to know Spanish, or be able to translate for a psychologist who has a Spanish-speaking only client. It's a bummer that I don't speak Spanish, because it is valuable to know Spanish in the medical field, because of much of the population we serve is Latino. For me it is frustrating that I cannot help and that someone else can be considered more valuable because they are bilingual.

I know who I am, but because of my genetics there is a certain expectation. It is just the way it is for later generations of Hispanics that come to America. They adapt and don't pass on the language because it was perceived as to serve their children better to learn English.

My daughter is the next generation, and her heritage, who she is, can be complicated. She has a light complexion and has dark blonde-brown hair. She looks less Hispanic than I did as a kid and she is 3/4ths Hispanic. My son looks like a Hispanic little boy, with a darker Mexican look. He has the black eyebrows, black hair and long black eye lashes. He is just an adorable little Mexican boy.

When my daughter was 6, she had to do a school project about where she came from. We raised my kids just plain American. We didn't identify people by their color or by their race. Where we were in Pasadena it is very diverse. I told my daughter, "Well, mommy is Spanish and German, and daddy is Mexican."

She says, "I'm Mexican!?"

We said, "Yeah."

She says, "I know Spanish?"

She totally thought she would know Spanish by being Mexican.

"No. Sorry."

We had to break it down to a 6 year old why she didn't know Spanish. This was not enough of an explanation and so she pretended she could speak Spanish using nonsense words, "Blah, blah, blah, bleh."

Now she's a freshman in high school and is taking Spanish. She wanted to drop the first day.

I said, "Well, you have people who can tutor you in Spanish, you don't have anyone that can tutor you in French or Mandarin. You're probably better off staying in Spanish."

After two weeks, she applied herself and began enjoying it. We've encouraged her learning, "Take this and then in your next semester take Spanish II. Learn it. Use it with friends, use it with people you know, learn it, because it's going to be an asset."

My culture is important to me, but in my family it is hard because I am constantly being torn to choose one part of me or the other. My mom's side would feel I was rejecting the white side if I identified myself as Hispanic. They do not understand that I can embrace the Hispanic and the white sides of my family. I don't have to choose one or the other. There is more colorful culture connected to my Latin side and that's what I identify with, and that is the side I really grew up with. My mother's side, while from German descent, lived in Oklahoma and did not celebrate that culture.

Because my lifestyle is more Hispanic, my friends are multi-cultural. I speak and connect to everyone because you can learn and grow from everybody. There's always something to better yourself from what you can take away from another culture. I haven't even raised my kids around just Hispanic people. I try to expose them to many cultures. I'm just American and I have a Hispanic background and a white background, but I'm still just an American.

Daniela's Story

Daniela's story is touching because she is a teacher and impacts the lives of many young children on a daily basis. Daniela is an immigrant too, and she arrived to the U.S. at a young age. Her story reflects the challenges of what some undocumented families have to deal with and I am proud that she allowed me to summarize her interview.

I am 40 years old and came to the United States when I was five. I was born in Tijuana. My parents always knew that living in Tijuana was just a pause on their journey to America. My family is originally from Guanajuato, which is near Guadalajara in Mexico, and that is where my two sisters were born. They knew they were going to come to the States, and so they began their journey. When they paused in Tijuana, my parents had me and my other sister.

My mother was basically a single mom while living in Tijuana, because my father travelled back and forth to the United States for work. He had a really hard time saving up the money that he needed to get us across the border. He wanted us to safely pass into America, and that took money. He did not want us in any danger.

I was considered to be illegal until I was about 15. When I was enrolled in school, I took my studies seriously. My goal was to learn and excel. I gained admission to study at an elite preparatory boarding school in New England and not until I was there did my paperwork to become a legal resident come through. I was thrilled and I was able to attain temporary citizenship. Even though I had the temporary status, and went to a boarding school, I was really not supposed to be in the U.S. I don't think my parents grasped that concept either.

I got to prep school because I had a wonderful counselor in junior high school. She had a daughter who she helped get into a prep school back East. Her daughter was three years ahead of me. The year she decided she was going to try to get her daughter into prep school, it opened that opportunity up to a few students that she counseled at our junior high school and encouraged them to apply. That began my school's first wave of Southern California kids who went back East.

The next year she opened up the process and my sister went through the process. Our counselor aligned herself with a program that was geared towards helping high achieving minority students apply to prep school. That program was called "A Better Chance." The process was that they sent a general application to a few boarding schools back East, and then those prep schools have an opportunity to decide who they think is the best fit for their schools.

It was 1989 when I went through the process and there were about five of us who were accepted. We all went to different schools, but we each were placed on a trajectory that would become life-changing for us. Without a doubt, this was a great opportunity because while my parents always instilled the value of education, they didn't know how to maneuver through much. I feel that I definitely needed to have some guidance and then a role model. I was determined to be college bound.

Even though I had the passion, I had no idea what I would major in college or really what I wanted to do. When I started college, I was just so excited to just be in college because I was the first one in my family to achieve that goal. While I was there, I had tunnel vision. I was focused on my education. I didn't know how to think beyond college because I was just so grateful that I was there. To me, success would have just been finishing college and calling it a day. Whereas other people who were there, they had a long-term plan. That long-term plan is the difference of when your parents know how to navigate the educational system compared to those parents like mine who were just delighted to have a child in college.

Several of my classmates knew they wanted to be lawyers, finance people, and doctors. I didn't have that guidance at the college level. When I was younger, I *had counselors who really kept an eye on us. At prep school, I had dorm heads who you checked in with on a day-to-day basis. When I gained my footing at college, I realized I could really misstep there. I needed to refocus and not just think about doing well in class but also think beyond college and how to pursue a career. While in elementary school and junior high school, my classmates faced the same social and economic struggles as my family experienced. We were all in the same boat. So our teachers made the extra effort to invest their time to help us and guide us as we battled through our daily lives. During high school, I was surrounded with resources, from teachers, counselors, coaches, and tutors that supported my endeavor, offered a shoulder to lean on when I needed emotional encouragement and helped my think two, three, and four steps ahead. At college, everyone is one their own.*

Of course we all have advisors, but an advisor is not a counselor. An advisor is there to help figure out which classes to take, but not necessarily there to help you think two, three or four steps ahead. In my experience, the folks that filled that role were the parents. The parents would advise their children, my classmates, which law/medical/graduate schools to apply and how to pursue life after college. My parents told me that I could come back home. While my parents were loving people, they did not know how to help me in this regard, so like most first generation Latino college students, I had to figure things out on my own.

Today, I am an educator. My experience, comparing both my public school and elite private school education has moved me to follow in the footsteps of the public school teachers who gave their all to help young minds like me. My students have the same family story as I do. I can relate to their struggles and try to serve as a role model to show that I too was raised in the same city, overcame the same obstacles and serve as proof that success is possible. However, it is obviously not so easy to change the mindset of students or, unfortunately, parents. When you just don't know how to navigate the channels, you have two options, 1) learn or 2) walk away. Many choose the latter.

I have 10 nieces and nephews and some of them are college age, but none of them have pursued college either. At some point something broke down in the system with that message that my parents had instilled in me about education. I believe I made it because I went to prep school. It gave me the skills and confidence to go and finish college.

Now I am a teacher. I felt, "What better way to shape young minds than working with children as a teacher?" I believe in helping others. I tutor a custodian that works at my school where I teach. I don't even know if he really has his high school diploma. I love working with him, because he wants to learn and never quits. He was too shy to really ask for help. Even with me when he approached me about this test he needs to take to move up in his job. He doesn't understand some of the math. I think it took a lot for him to reach out to me.

I had encouraged him because I had sat down with other people who had wanted to move up in their jobs too. I always want to be that inspirational teacher who guides my students that are under my watch. But for me, it goes beyond that.

If I have a grown 50-some year old man who knows I'm a teacher and I know he's about to study for something that may be a little difficult for him, I want to help him anyway I can. I think for me that's really rewarding to know that I have that type of rapport and influence with my students to know that other adults my age, older than me also feel comfortable enough to really reach out. To me, it reassures me that what I'm doing is worth doing and I am serving the role to help my students think two, three, four steps ahead.

Excy's Story

Her name is pronounced Ex-See and I was introduced to her through a mutual friend because I asked him to help me find a Latina I could interview to discuss how she got to America. Excy's story inspires and I want to share her words with you.

I was born in Honduras and I remember being hungry all the time. I didn't have things that I take for granted now – things like shoes. I did not understand my life then like I understand looking back on it now. When no one has anything around you, then you do not notice the things you don't have. It is just your normal life. I loved running around and just playing in the dirt.

My parents did know we were poor and they wanted more for us. In an effort to simply do something, my father made the gut wrenching decision to leave us and find work in the U.S. I was 3 years old when my father began his journey and from how he described it, the journey was treacherous and he almost. There are a million ways to die crossing the border.

Once he made it, he sent for my mother, then my bother and then finally I was brought over, when I was 5 years old. I was living with my grandmother in Honduras and I would constantly ask her when my mother and father were coming home. It's expensive to pay for the border crossing, so obviously we all had to be patient until we were called. To bring me over, my parents were searching for people who specialized in helping kids across the border, but even then, the trip remained dangerous and many kids never made it across.

My parents found a woman who agreed to take me across. For several years, I have tried to find her to thank her, because her courage reunited me with my family. However, when I was in high school, I learned that she was caught by the authorities for helping kids like me find a new beginning and she went underground, cutting off all communication.

This woman had her processes mapped out. Her specialty was getting children across the border by flying on an airplane. To achieve this, she falsified documents and pretended she was the child's parent. She would coach the children how to behave and what to say when they would board the plane. One morning, my grandmother told me that a woman was coming to take me to my parents. I can still remember being picked up by her and my grandma saying to me, "This woman is going to take you to see your mom."

I was ecstatic, but at the same time confused about what was happening. I quickly stuffed what meager belongings I had, like clothes and my toys, into a bag and got into her car. I did not know where we were going, but I do remember that the drive was long. What I eventually learned when I got older was that the she took me to a drop house in Guatemala, a neighboring country of Honduras.

I remember arriving at a place where there were more adults and a group of 10-15 children all around my same age. We stayed there for some time. We would eat together and shower together, but we had to stay inside the house.

When the day came to finally board the plane and make our way to the U.S., the woman told me that she was giving me a new name to use. I would get really mad and be like no, my name is Excy. When we arrived to the airport, we walk to our gate and waited for the boarding process to begin. When the boarding process did begin, we were in line, waiting for our turn to go on the airplane. The woman and her male companion were pretending to be my parents and I almost blew our cover when ticket agent took our boarding passes. The woman told the agent when we were boarding the plane that they were my parents and gave the agent my "new name." I became even angrier and said loudly that my name was Excy and that I was going to see my mom. The woman told the agent I was having a temper tantrum and we boarded the plane.

It was not cheap for my parents to get me to the U.S. It cost between $5,000 and $6,000 per child to get them across the border, which is why there was a lag time getting me here. My parents worked day and night literally for months. They knew the conditions that I was living in and they wanted to get me out of there as soon as they could.

They constantly worked and did not sleep much and by the time I saw them, they looked like zombies. I landed in Houston. Soon thereafter, my parents decided to move the entire family to northern Virginia because there were more opportunities for work.

I grew up in Arlington, Virginia. When I started school my family told me not to tell anyone where I was from or how I got here. I did not know what undocumented meant, but keeping that secret made me feel different from everyone else. As I grew older I understood it more and have endured many hardships because of being undocumented. I was treated differently at school.

It was no easier for my parents. They were janitors and had to put up with a lot because they were undocumented. I remember one time, I got my mom fired because I stood up to her boss, who was talking down to her. My mother could take it, but I couldn't. It was just not right to treat another person that way.

When I was ready to go to college, I was told I couldn't continue because I couldn't get my papers. I was told, "People like you can't go to college."

I couldn't afford to go on my own. I have lived here most of my life and now I was being treated like a throw-away. I was very upset, but I didn't give up. I told the teachers my story and they honored me with a full tuition scholarship, which they don't give to undocumented students. They gave me the full tuition scholarship and I was able to complete college.

Jesse A. Mejia

Even though I have lived in the U.S. for 20 years and have graduated college, I still only have a temporary protective status (TPS), which means I have a work permit and a Social Security number to work. It also allows me to get a driver's license, so that I can work. The problem is that it means I am still deportable. It's not based on how long you've been here, rather it is based on what laws are in place. I came here illegally, so that alone makes it difficult for me to have a legal status. It did not stop me from getting an education and working, but it still a dark cloud that hangs over me.

It has also prevented me from ever returning to the country I was born. There is a special permit that would allow me to leave the country if I was on a trip with a school or on a mission trip or some other extreme situation. Even though I could have applied I am too scared to leave because what if I can't come back in?

My college major was International Global Studies, and one of the requirements of that major was that I was to study abroad. I ran into trouble and had to explain to my school why I couldn't leave the country. The school worked with me after I explained my situation. I decided to do a project to make up for not studying abroad.

Unfortunately, TPS is not a pathway to citizenship. It's something that we renew every year and pay between $450 and $600 for the permit. Protecting your temporary status is critically important because there is no tolerance for any misconduct. For instance, if anyone would let their TPS expire and subsequently had any type of DUI or anything on their record, those missteps would be sufficient to consider deportation.

A few years ago, my uncle let his TPS expire. He had two or three DUIs, and immigration came and raided our entire house and took him. He couldn't legally say he had the TPS. The officers knocked on the door, but I was prepared because I knew what my rights are. It was four in the morning, and some us were ready to go to work. They began pounding on the door and everyone woke up. My uncle ran upstairs and told us that Immigration was there. He was so scared he did not know what to do. We kept telling him, "Open the door, open the door."

At this point they had surrounded our house. There were there in full gear in their black unmarked cars and their guns were drawn like they were ready to take someone very dangerous down.

My uncle opened the door and they flooded my house. They went into every single room. They told us to come sit downstairs, they turned on all the lights. They asked each person their name, their date of birth and our status.

While we were waiting to be questioned, we were talking amongst each other deciding what we should say. They asked my dad, "Where are your documents? Where's your family's documents?"

My dad is not really good at keeping things organized. He became panicked trying to find his TPS card. It took a really long time for him to find it, while the rest of the family was worried about what they would do if he did not find his card.

The immigration officers were laughing and making jokes. I felt totally invaded and angry that they could just come in my house do whatever they wanted. We hadn't done anything wrong.

They had been to our house before and so they had a list of who had stayed with us or who had rented rooms. They began asking questions like, "Where is this person? Are you sure you don't know? If you're lying to us you're going to be in trouble. You need to tell us where they are."

When they got to my uncle, things did not go well for him. "We have here that you have a record of a couple DUIs. You don't have current documentation and so we will have to take you with us." My uncle is one of those macho people who never shows emotion. When they began handcuffing him, he began to cry. He said to my father, "Take care of my things. Can you send my things to me? Take care of my things." After they took him that day, we never heard from my uncle again.

Today, I am an English as a Second Language teacher. I help children like me find their space and courage so they can cope with their situation. While I am still battling through my own issues, I feel compelled to help shine some hope in the lives of children that suffered like me. I understand the laws, but I was brought here as a minor. This is my home and this is the home of my students. No one aspires to live unlawfully, not my students, not me and not the parents who brought us here. I understand that the actions that my parents took was illegal, but I was too young to even make a decision. Most children had no say on whether or not to come to the U.S. Nevertheless, we are here now. I encourage my students to excel academically. I teach them about respect, professionalism, and work ethic. I illustrate for them that they way to gain success in this country is by being educated, *ambitious, and making sure you have friends to help you along the way. I do my best to lead by example and I am committed to empowering them to become educated contributors to the American society.*

Irene's Story

Irene's story is special because she comes from a political family. The country of Colombia has always had its economic and social challenges and this why Irene's family decided to leave politics so they could provide for their children to grow up in a more stable government. Here is Irene's story, in her own words.

My parents are from Colombia. In the 1980s, my grandmother worked for the Colombian government. There was a lot of corruption going on around her, and for a time she had to go into hiding. In the end, she got cleared of any issues, but after that my mom wanted to leave the country. She could not stand living there anymore. She said to me, "There was no future there unless you're cheating or doing something bad, but in the end you're going to be locked up or dead."

My dad had a similar story and he also wanted to leave because of all the corruption. They came to the U.S. with tourist visas and as soon as they expired, they started the immigration process immediately.

They met in early 1990, and were married. They both decided they had a better future here, but their immigration process became so messed up. They tried to do things legally but got into issues with their employers. They were stuck in limbo for almost 16 years. They were not illegal, but they weren't residents or citizens of the United States, either.

Every day for them was, "What's going to happen?" There was actually a point when I was in middle school, where my mom's lawyer called up and he told her, "It's now or never. We are going to have to basically pull out a Hail Mary here, and see if you are going to be able to stay."

That was maybe the scariest moment in my whole life, because I was in a point where we were pretty sure that we were going to have to leave. And I had never been to Colombia, I didn't even speak that much Spanish, and my brother much less.

We did get past this scare and I am happy to say that my parents are true citizens now. We grew up in New York, and fortunately my brother and I never really faced any big race issues or immigration issues because we were lucky enough that we look kind of ethnically ambiguous and our parents raised us speaking both English and Spanish.

When I was young I was tested for my hearing and because I didn't speak too much and it turned out it was because I was used to hearing both languages so much that I wasn't sure which one I should speak in at which time. After they tested me my parents said, "Oh, no, no, no. There's nothing wrong with her. She's really smart. She speaks English and Spanish. She's just wondering which one she should be speaking to you guys."

People like to use the term anchor babies around my brother and me, but we are far from that reality. Our parents came here for us and their intentions were to stay in the country. When my mother became pregnant with me is when they decided they really wanted to stay here, otherwise she probably would have given up and gone back instead of being stuck in limbo with her employer. My parents worked hard so that we wouldn't grow up the way a lot of first generation people do here where they're still struggling to improve their lives in this country.

My brother and I want to show that there's a reason that we're here, and be active enough to show there's a reason that the immigration process has to change in this country because there are good people who want to be here and make a change. I'm getting my master's in public policy so that I'll be able to help out people who need it in this country.

In my junior year of high school, I was part of a program that allowed me to take college classes. I was able to graduate with college credits. Early in the program, I approached my teacher and asked why there were so few minorities in the class. She replied, "Well that's because most of them don't even have papers." And she just dismissed it that way. This did not seem right – if a child in school could qualify and do the work they should be allowed to participate. For the most part, they were just being dismissed before they were allowed a chance.

I was part of a program "Opportunity Awareness," and so I reached out to kids from different schools and their parents. I told them, "You're not from here and you don't know how this process works. Let me tell you what you can do. These are lists of scholarships, organizations, places that your kids can go to and they can have the opportunity to continue their education."

Even in my own home, my parents did not know what it took for me to be able to go to college. I was researching how to do it since I was in middle school. The process was easier for my brother because my mom already had the information packages. The process is easy as long as you know what you are doing, but when you are from another country you don't always know where to start.

I worked hard and was able to graduate college in three years, even though right before I graduated high school, I was diagnosed with a tumor in my head. I decided I needed to go anyway, I already put in all the hard work, so it wasn't going to stop me. The tumor was benign, but it still affected me every day. I just concentrated on my work while I was in college, and so I did not join many organizations like I would have liked too, but I knew I had this opportunity and I did not want anything to get in my way.

I did however join a local Latino elected officials group because I wanted to get more involved with politics. Getting involved helped me network with the right people and I sought out some of the members to become my mentors. One of my mentors actually took me to my first meeting with him for lunch, and I share with him that I approached him because I overheard him say that he graduated from Syracuse University and that Syracuse was my dream school. I told him. "I'm applying right now. I'm so excited."

He stopped me right there and said "Irene, this is my card, as soon as you send your application in, you let me know." He wrote me a recommendation letter. I have had so many more opportunities just because of my involvement and ability to network with others.

I still struggle with my health issues, but I have committed to helping others access services, especially Latinos, who have no idea how to apply for things. Achieving success is about having a vision and a roadmap to achieve that vision. Many parents don't have either because they are focused on today only. Whether it's going to college, graduate school or your career after college, it all starts with a vision and then developing a path. I believe in the power of roadmaps and now it has become my life's mission to help others create their roadmaps so they too can achieve success.

Overcoming Hardship

The reason I shared these specific personal stories, is because these are the stories that represent our Latino history in America. Over the past 10 years, I have spoken to, coached, mentored or advised more than 1,000 Latinos on how they should pursue their professional development. While most are enthusiastic about striving for a life in Corporate America, few actually follow through on pursuing a professional career. I say *RISE UP, MI GENTE* because I believe we can do better. I share the stories from Mario, Luis, Jocelyn, Daniela, Excy, and Irene to prove a point that we all have to overcome a level of hardship. Not everyone can have the same path to success because not everyone started at the same place in life.

Whether you are a recent arrival or a Latino who does not speak Spanish, we are still *a community*. We, as a community can limit our ambition because we are so focused on what we are facing today, the problems we are dealing with right now. I get it! We live in the moment, but we cannot have tunnel vision. As Daniela shared in her story, we need to be thinking two, three, four steps ahead. I selected each story because each contributes a different element to the struggle and each provides a unique glimpse on how they tackled their struggle. All went college, some have advanced degrees, but each is Rising Up.

Overcoming hardship is not an overnight success story. It requires time, vision, and commitment. Create your roadmap and stay the course.

CHAPTER 5

Being a Latino Leader in the 21ˢᵗ Century

• • •

BEING A LATINO LEADER IS no easy task. I went to people I knew who were successful Latino business leaders, and while many of their answers I expected, some of their answers took me by surprise. As a Latino in Corporate America, I already knew that it is a struggle to get to high positions. In this world, we accept the fact that at times it's isolating because there are those who just choose not to engage with us. But that's okay. We have learned how to deal with those personalities. The never-ending challenge is that every day, day in and day out, we need to prove that we are not the unqualified token Latino who was graciously placed on the path for a high-level position because the company is trying to be a better corporate citizen and prove to the world that it believes in diversified workforce. For us, the margin of error is much smaller, simply because the expectations for the quality of our work is not always assumed to be high.

The irony here is that most Fortune 500 corporations have call centers. These call centers are where customer service departments reside. These are also the entry-level jobs of where many corporations choose to develop their talent pool. I started my career at a call center and many Latinos who have careers in Corporate America did too. The problem comes when Latinos do not know how to move beyond the call center, and that's simply because there is no one there to teach us how. There is no shortage of leadership skills within the Latino community. Many of us were leaders in school, holding executive leadership roles with our student clubs, fraternities/ sororities, or other extracurricular activity. So the question then becomes, why there aren't more Latinos in positions of corporate management?

Through my interviews, the revelation came when one said, *"In order for there to be a place at the table for all Latino leaders, Latinos who have paved the way must be willing to offer a hand up."* Discrimination occurs in voids, when there are not enough people to stand up. When there are more Latinos as leaders within an organization, the conversation and culture change. The only thing Latinos should be afraid of is being in isolation. We are not tokens, we are qualified men and woman who can compete at the highest levels. We need to find opportunities to showcase our skills and be mindful to help one another when possible. I stress that we need to help each other because when we are not at the table, we do not have a voice. When there are not enough of us at the table, then we can get drowned out. Latinos must help more Latinos become competitive and provide the encouragement so we can compete at the executive levels.

Navigating your career has challenges. There will always be a person or people who just make life difficult. No one is immune from dealing with these types of individuals, but there are ways to figure it out. The best way I can share with you how other Latinos navigate their corporate careers is by continuing to share with you their story in their own words.

I will highlight two stories for you, Tomas and Javier. Both worked for Fortune 500 Corporation and both had to overcome distinct challenges that will help you figure out how to create your own solutions when you are faced with similar problems. Both stories in this chapter represent not only successes but the real struggles Latino leaders face, often in silence, every day.

Tomas' Story

I have known Tomas for more than 20 years. His business acumen is strong, his pride in his Mexican heritage is strong, and his ability to navigate his career is also strong. Tomas' story on how he was able to find success with three different Fortunate 500 companies, especially in a setting that did not have many people who looked like him is a perspective I want to share with you. I appreciate his story as a business leader, his professional experience, and I believe his insight is suitable for anyone who is either in the early stages of their career or a seasoned professional ready to change careers. Here is Tomas story in his own words.

I grew up in sunny California – Burbank to be specific – which is on the other side of Hollywood in L.A. Both sides of my family originally came from Mexico. My dad's family emigrated from Guadalajara. My mom's family was originally from Chihuahua. Both sides of my family are first generation American.

They grew up in a small industrial town, many people there worked for the movie and T.V. studios. I grew up with public education and placed well academically and athletically, which earned my entrance into the University of Pennsylvania. I originally wanted to go to school for business.

I really didn't have much to go on other than the fact that my parents demanded that each of their three boys either get a job or go to college upon turning 18. Both my parents were high school dropouts, but they wanted more for us. My older brother decided to test out and graduated high school early. He went on to have a successful career. I was going to go to college, which was about as much as I knew.

I was very fortunate though, as my best friend's dad was a successful businessman. He was asking those questions nobody else knew to ask me about school and I told him I wanted to go in business. He was the one who introduced me to the Wharton School at the University of Pennsylvania and the fact that they were one of the few schools that had both a renowned undergraduate business program as well as a prestigious MBA program. My friend's father really helped prepare me for the college applications and entrance interviews. He was not Latino, but he liked my parents and me and decided to provide guidance. It would have definitely been a lot harder in terms of translating my thoughts and my capabilities as a high school applicant without his support.

One night I went to dinner at their home while my friend's uncle was in town. We were having a great time. His uncle got to know me and my story a bit over dinner and he made the remark that my parents must be so proud of me in achieving above and beyond my race. It was an awkward moment, and my friend and his father came to my defense, and his uncle tried to turn it around, but it was left hanging out there. The more I thought about it the more I stewed on it and it really made me mad.

A few days later, my friend's dad pulls me aside, "I just want you to know it doesn't matter how you were born, you've earned everything you got. That's how good you are, that's how smart you are, that's how hard you've worked. I promise you everybody in this family values you for who you are and what you've done."

While not my first experience with subtle, yet racist comments, I still did not know how to process those situations back when I was 18 years old. In time I learned. Mostly because I experienced those comments more often. When you are one of the few Latinos in your circle, because you are able to compete at higher levels, sometimes your reward is dealing with the ignorance of people who look nothing like you but have solutions for how your community can do better. Dealing with issues of race or what not at the work place or in society sometimes requires you to deal with it straight on, but other times you need to handle it with discretion and diplomacy. You don't have to handle the confrontation just because someone comes at you with ignorance.

I had to learn to eloquently articulate myself and use what I would say is my cultural strength of being Latino. Using your Latino culture can either really work for you or really work against you in terms of being plain spoken and being passionate.

During my junior year in college, I had the opportunity to intern with Proctor & Gamble, a leading consumer packaged goods company. One of my roommates had gone through the supply chain intern program for the company the year before and he shared his experience. He raved about it and, after listening to the things he got to do, the places he got to travel, and the types of problem-solving he got involved with, I was sold.

With his help, I networked effectively with many executives at that company and I was picked for an internship. I knocked it out the park during my time there and received an offer to come back after graduating with my degree, I completed my undergraduate degree in economics that next year and shortly thereafter began my career with P&G's purchasing department.

Even though I wasn't buying anything exotic, I was buying packaging materials for men's and women's deodorant, I was in an environment that was teaching me how to be a critical thinker in a corporate setting. What my parents had hoped for me, I was beginning to accomplish and my family felt proud. My parents gloated when I would tell them about the cutting edge technology that I was exposed to, that fact that I came dressed in a suit every day and that I also participated in the wheeling and dealing of products with all these people at other major companies. My whole job was to get the best values in matchups in cost, quality and performance to support my employer in its mission to serve its customers. This experience brought out my best in terms of sharpening my skill sets. That foundation of wheeling and dealing has helped me create a 20-plus-year career in buying/ supply chains.

As my career progressed, I reached a point where I wanted to grow further and I decided that I was ready to leave my employer, so I began looking for new opportunities. I had learned so much and had made some great connections, but I was ready to grow, and the position I was in just was not going to allow me to do that.

I came across two great job offers, one from American Airlines and one from Delta Airlines. Planes seemed to be a very exciting new area to work in. I had the opportunity to visit both locations, one in Dallas, Texas, and one in Atlanta, Georgia.

When I went to Dallas, I had a great experience. There were many people who looked like me, and who were Spanish like me. In Atlanta, there was very little visibility of anything Latino. The few Mexican restaurants for the most part served everything with ground beef. I had to tell people that's not really Mexican food, and as a proud Mexican-American, I was stunned how this was even enjoyable. Nevertheless, I had to do some soul searching and decided that while Dallas felt almost like home, Atlanta was the place I needed to be. People ask me why I did not choose American Airlines. You would think that would be a better fit for me culturally and personally.

There were two things that ultimately drove me to choose Delta. First, the gentleman who built the purchasing department at American had just recently moved to Delta. They were rebuilding the organization from the ground up. Their sell to me was you can come on as a buyer and put your stamp on it and help us rebuild our organization. The second thing was during my interview process with American I had interviewed with nine people. Out of those nine people, one person was a fellow Latino. The recruiter shared with me very positive reviews, he said "people liked you." There was just one person who expressed some skepticism. That interviewer said that I was well-spoken and well read. Was I really that good or did I just prepare well?

I found out that the person who had doubts was the Latino.

My thought process was that I didn't want to be in place where Latinos felt like they had to compete with each other for a spot. I'm not interested in taking anyone's spot. I'm trying to make my own spot. While small, the reaction was significant to me. I wanted to grow in a team environment that was based on trust and acceptance. So I went with my gut and that's what drove me to make my final decision to go to Delta. Moreover, it was also that experience that motivated me to help other Latinos with their career. I made sure I was viewed as a resource, not as a competitor, because I believe that we must help each other out.

My career at Delta flourished. I was with Delta almost ten years and I was moving up through the ranks. It was a fabulous time being in the industry and helping out the organization. I refined my management skills and leadership abilities, but most of all, I learned how to manage people. I found great pride serving in the role of a mentor, giving back in ways that were afforded to me. However, what I loved most about my team is that I was supported in my desires to strive for more. Unlike those in my old company, I had to figure out how not to feel as if I was being disloyal if I wanted to further my skills at a different company. In time, I learned how to deal with that emotion and soon thereafter, a recruiter came to me with an opportunity with Alaskan Airlines with a very similar scenario to the one that brought me to Delta. However, this opportunity was at the director level! I had told myself I wanted to progress with my career and now I had a chance to compete for a larger role, admittedly with a smaller company. Nevertheless, I *was being sold on the ability to help shape and rebuild the organization directly. Opportunities to be "the Guy" come along only so often, so I took a leap of faith and decided to accept that opportunity. I left my adopted home of Atlanta and came to the Pacific Northwest where I spread my wings even further and soared into another successful 10-year career run.*

While I am proud of what I have accomplished, I want to temper my positive experience by also sharing some of the challenges I had to overcome. There were a couple of encounters on top of the business challenges that I had to figure out resolutions for, and they had nothing to do with the caliber of my work. When I worked for the consumer packaged goods company, I came to feel as if I was a Latino who was an employee a bit under the microscope. It was just that extra burden to feel that there were a few extra eyes on me. It was that weird feeling of "You're not one of us but you're kind of one of us" where you are an employee, but not part of the circle. I had to address off-colored jokes that were made by coworkers at the expense of Mexicans. Many times, I had to bite my lip and learn to accept that in my corporate world, I was outnumbered and could not risk making a scene without it impacting my livelihood. I had to pick my battles. When I did decide to speak up, I was told that I was overreacting, which I later learned that was simply another form of micro aggression to make me seem like I was the alpha male with the hot Mexican temper. While I left that company because I wanted to further my career, the quiet voice in my head had told me to start looking so I would not lose my sanity. An aspect of achieving success is also having the self-awareness to know when it's time to leave on your own terms.

When I was at Delta, I was just an employee that happened to be Latino. I felt good there and nothing got so out of line that I was not able to address it alone through a simple man-to-man conversation. I enjoyed Delta, its corporate culture and the people. When I got to Alaska Airlines, I originally had the feeling of being an employee that happened to be Latino because of the fact that at Alaska, the leadership looked past the diversity issue all together. That was neither a good thing nor a bad thing, but rather I just found myself working in an environment that was color-blind. Before I joined the company, Alaska decided to make attracting diverse employees a bigger company focus, so the few people who looked like me were all actually recruited by the top company brass. It absolutely gave the impression that the company was serious about its hiring strategy. Alaska needed talented, diverse employees to help them become a better and a more successful company by sharing perspectives and tackling business problems from angles that they were not accustomed to, such as me leveraging the purchasing processes I learned from my Proctor & Gamble and Delta Airlines. Similar to managing individual personalities, companies also have their own distinctive personalities, referred to as corporate culture. I have had the good fortune to be gainfully employed by three different Fortune 500 companies, but my third experience was my most eye-opening experience because my personal upbringing of being Latino and being an upfront and candid individual now became my Achilles heel. At Alaska, I felt that I could not be me. I was now surrounded by what I perceived to be a high number of passive aggressive people and I struggled on how to react. There were decisions made that I did not agree with, and enough cultural insensitivity that I could not always ignore. However, I had learned my lesson from my experience at Proctor & Gamble that sometimes, it is best to just walk away. Temperance was something I definitely had to practice. It challenged who I was inside both personally and culturally, and I had to work hard to adjust and adapt to my environment. In the summer of 2014, I decided to begin a new chapter in my professional life and chose to work for a smaller company, still focuses in aerospace, but in an environment where I could be 100% an educated, professional, American-born Mexican.

Fitting in as a Latino

Now, as an American-born Mexican, how did I make my way to fit in? Whether you grow up in New York, Chicago, Miami, San Antonio, or Los Angeles like me, I believe that the one thing that Latino households have in common is that we are loud and we are passionate. We want to help, we work hard, great work ethic, but on some level we want to enjoy what we do. That did not mean everyone understood or accepts that culture. I was in a big city and it was a different culture. People were very polite and measured. My parents advised me, "You've got to fit in. You've got to take care of your boss ... tell him thank you often and do what you can for him. Don't be too loud. Don't do your Cinco de Mayo celebration and try to share it with everyone. Celebrate and do that outside of work. You need to blend in. Just fit in with the company."

I was getting the same kinds of messages at work about what they expected me to act like and be like. I was about 23, and said to myself "Is this what the next forty to fifty years of my life are going to be like, fitting in?"

There are parts of my heritage and culture that people who knew me best loved, but I couldn't be that way at work? It was difficult to be two people.

When I went to Delta, it was different because most of the issues of culture were between blacks and whites. I was perceived to be on the white side there. I was less threatening to my Caucasian colleagues and my African American colleagues got a kick out of it.

There's a story about me standing up on the desk to make a point to a supplier with poor performance, trying to tell us how it was going to be. I said, "I am literally standing on my desk and I have now interrupted all of my colleagues because this is your last opportunity to get money from my company, the end." I could be more myself.

Then when I went to Alaska Airlines and it started with my boss saying to me that I needed to be kinder and gentler. I responded that I did not want to feel like I had to quit being who I am in order to be successful. That's hard. Isn't there a third option where I can hone who I am in a way which is more plausible for the company, which still gives me the opportunity to perform at my peak and do the best for the company? That's probably something I continue to work on in my almost 12 years here in the Pacific Northwest.

Preserving who I was came in the form of outlets. What I mean by "outlets," I was seeking out anywhere I could go, or any type of cultural celebrations that would occur in the places that I lived. I needed a space to be me. Whether that space was mentoring grade school kids in Cincinnati or coaching youth baseball and soccer teams when I was Atlanta, I sought my spaces. I also wanted to help academically, so when I got to Seattle, I would mentor students at the high school and collegiate level. I volunteered on my fraternity's national leadership and helped expand our organization. These activities helped me stay active and live the aspects of my life that were important to me.

I do things that keep me in touch and attuned with not just my culture but other cultures as well. I jokingly say that the one way that a Latino can ensure *acceptance in Corporate America is by taking advantage of every potluck opportunity possible. When you bring in some authentic enchiladas or tamales or something that people haven't had before, with just enough spice, (but not too much spice), people respond, "Oh my gosh! Give me the recipe. Oh my gosh, that's amazing! Oh my gosh, you've got to bring those in again." Food breaks down barriers whenever I see either a lack of understanding, neglect, or misunderstandings between people. I can knock some enchiladas out of the park. Whether or not you get along with me afterwards may be a work in progress, but at least my food is good.*

Regardless of where you work, Fortune 500 or not, in life, you will always come across ignorance. While some may be innocent, others may just be cruel. Nevertheless, as Latinos, we are the ones trying to break in and it is our job to find ways to fit in. If it doesn't work, it was not because you did not try, but try you must. One of the best pieces of advice I received on how to fit it was when my first boss at Delta pulled me to the side and told me what I could do to fit into the South and the way Southern Boys think.

My boss was born and raised right outside of Atlanta. His main advice to me, to be successful, was simply two parts. "Know what you're coming with. You're a supply chain guy. You're going to help teach us how to buy as a company. You don't have to prove that to anyone, just help people. Reach out to people and be helpful and supportive to people."

The second piece he said, in terms of just being successful as a guy who is not from the South. I was not homegrown within Delta, and at that time Delta had some turnover and people like me, people not from the South, were often treated like outsiders.

The way my boss approached me was in a pleasant and supportive manner. He said, "Hey, Tomas, do you like NASCAR?"

I said, "Yeah, I've watched NASCAR, I'm more of an NHRA guy, somewhat less."

He goes, "That's okay, how about football? Do you like football?"

I replied, "Like professional teams?"

He goes, "No, no, college football- SEC."

"I know of the SEC conference."

He was serious when he replied, "Here's the thing, Tomas, I'm not suggesting that you become a NASCAR fan, and not suggesting that you become a fanatic picking SEC team. What I am telling you is that there are a lot people in the South, and there are a lot of people in this company who personally live and die with their favorite driver or their favorite team. Whether or not they went to school there does not matter. A lot of the conversations that help people get to know each other and build the trust, to open things up as they do business together, is based upon being able to connect to each other through those things. What I'm suggesting you do is, whether or not you're a fan, watch ESPN over the weekend, go online on Monday and read what team played and who won. Understand some of the story lines, know what driver won the race. Know whether they were out that weekend. Just know enough so that you can reach out and participate in those conversations as they happen around the office place. As you do that people will stop thinking about you as the guy from the college up north who is originally from California, who is an off-product from that fancy Proctor & Gamble company. They will simply think of you as one of their own and they will treat you like one of their own and you will be that much more successful, and you will help us be more successful."

My boss' words were deep. I took his advice to heart. As an avid Los Angeles Lakers and Raiders fan, I could relate to their love for SEC football. NASCAR I had to learn, much like I would expect someone to learn if they came to my hometown and ignored the love our community had for soccer. Much like the Latino culture, we build everything on trust. The relationships and the trust are that much more paramount between people in businesses. The ability to reach out and to commit the effort to understand people from their perspective, their culture, what they're into, and their regional interests is not a foreign concept to me. I just had to make the effort to understand their culture. I made the effort to understand what "Roll Tide" meant, the history of the SEC rivalries such as Auburn vs. Georgia or Georgia vs Florida, and I also read up on NASCAR legends like Dale Earnhardt, Jeff Gordon and Rusty Wallace. In doing so, I learned about them and they asked me more about me. In being able to share a little bit about yourself so they can learn and get to know you is tremendous in terms of building that foundation. And once they start sharing stories about themselves, you are creating bonds with people that have the potential to be your allies and champions. You want people to say good things about you when you are not in the room. Making the effort to fit into your corporation's culture is a great way to achieve success.

To Have an MBA or Not

I don't have an MBA. As far as opportunities within the companies I've worked for I don't know that not having an MBA has hurt me or hindered my trajectory or upward mobility. I do think not having that accreditation or having an MBA may have some level of impact in terms of the number of opportunities a Latino may have to continue to move up to a VP level job for a company. In some cases, I have seen people given VP roles and then be sent to an executive MBA program.

For young Latinos, given the opportunity, I do believe you should pursue an MBA. It maximizes your growth and upward movement. Just like growing up without a college degree, it doesn't mean you couldn't be successful but there may be a point where you would probably plateau. My situation was different, given the fact that when I started in my profession, supply chain was an underutilized skill and I was able to flourish in environments that were still building those departments

Does Discrimination Really Occur?

One of the companies I worked for had socialization times with new potential hires in which they were introduced to established people in the company. It was a happy hour event and it was their time to network internally to get to know some of the company's movers and shakers. There was this young recruit who had attended Harvard. His dad was a long-time executive of the company. We went into the reception with all these directors and General Managers. This new guy, he was a rock star; this guy was better known than the president. He had privilege and that played out in the mixer. He was an SOB. He would say disparaging things about women, refer to diversity quotas when he saw minority employees and was always had odd remarks such as, "what about us white guys?"

I immediately did not get along with this guy because of his off-color jokes, sexist jokes and Mexican jokes. He had invited one of his buddies to the social and they were questioning everybody's sexuality and they were bumping and pushing each other and they were bumping and pushing me.

I was asked to drop this guy off at house because he had too much to drink. In the back of my mind, I was thinking, "If a Latino pulled this stunt, he would be out of here." Nevertheless, I had to go with the flow. While I was driving, the kid became even more belligerent with me and pushed me into the steering wheel. I refused to deal with this guy any further, so I hit the brakes, we both got out the car and brawled until he gave up. While he got the worst of it that night, I should have known better because this guy was connected throughout the company and had far more leverage than me.

As far as the company was concerned he basically got a pass, but I was brought in and I was told I should retain a lawyer because this was going to be investigated and I could lose my job and be sued. I told my boss that I was not trying to be fired but I had no problem standing before a court and explaining what went down. I also reminded them I would also have to tell the court about another employee that had left the company and on her exit interview advised the company for what she felt was harassment of the Latinas within the company. She had specified a particular company-sponsored event that she had gone to with a couple other Latinos and they were subjected to a lot of racial jokes and epithets and she filed a complaint within HR in the company. It never went anywhere and she decided, "You know, this is not the place for me to work."

I was prepared to speak in front of a judge and not just my own experience but in sharing these other experiences that I was aware of. I was neither fired nor was I sued. I was moved on to a new boss and from the first day I worked with that new boss, every single little thing that my new boss did not like I was pulled into her office and was written up as poor work habits and categorized as performance issues. I complained that how could my work be construed as poor when my same approach to my job had not changed, with the exception of my boss, and that I was now viewed as an underachiever. My complaint with our human resources department fell on deaf ears. I had once heard that employees don't quit companies, they quit managers and because of the blatant disregard to human decency amongst their employees of color, I decided to resign.

While discrimination does exist, in my opinion, we will never get away from it because we are human beings. As a Latino, my suggestion is to recognize it, but don't let it consume you. You still have to earn a living. While you may not want to work for a company that has people like this, you will never be able to escape it. If your ambition is to achieve success in Corporate America, you will need to deal with racism, and that's okay. The higher you go up the corporate ladder, the less Latinos you will find. Our community is not there yet where we can have massive numbers serving in C-Suite roles, but without people like you to try to become C-Suite executives, the corporate culture will never change. Discrimination is alive and well, but so are you. Just Rise Up!

Javier's Story

I chose to interview Javier because of his tenure at work and the global assignments that he has had to lead. Travelling the world is an aspect of work that many of my friends would aspire to do. However, volunteering in your home community was also a priority. Making the time to volunteer would be limited, and at times, we would get criticized for not making the community a priority. This goes back to my earlier comment that I believe we as Latinos need to give when we are in a position of strength. I want to share Javier's story and how he balanced his career with his community involvement.

I've been at BP for ten years and before that, I worked for an insurance company for six years, always based in Chicago. The insurance company was an old-school, suspenders, tie, kind of organization that only caters to big businesses. BP is an oil company that has been around for over a hundred years and is based out of the U.K. Two very stereotypical companies that hire the best. In the case of the insurance company they hire talented people who can be actuaries. Actuaries are math folks that understand the probability of risk, these folks study how to price insurance and their whole job is to make the insurance company money. At

BP, they like people who are top of the line engineers who can work in one of their units and either help find oil or help process it.

From the career opportunity standpoint, what's very tough is if you're a Latino in that market, whether you're supporting the engineers or supporting the actuaries, that it is a very different world from the people who work in the public sector and maybe even other companies because the ladder to climb and work through is, in my opinion, much tougher. Both industries are industries that may not understand the struggle of an immigrant, the struggle of a Latino, or the struggle of an inner city person who has to work a little bit differently than the people who may have had all the education, the background, the opportunities, and maybe the guidance to really get to where they're at. It's a different mindset and it's a different working culture, as well, too.

I think it's an opportunity because if you really want to understand why somebody continues, why I, a Latino, continue to work in a Fortune 500 company and really want to achieve greatness is that we have a different drive. The concept – or actually the pressure we always work against – is, have we sold out? I think it's a very different picture that we paint when we're saying we worked hard, we do what we do because we believe in what we're doing. We don't think we're selling out, it's just a whole different ball game, when it comes to working in the corporate sector versus working for a non-profit.

Selling Out

Growing up in an inner city, we always had to compete. We have the pressures against us. I lived in a bad neighborhood. I had gangs and drugs, and my parents worked hard to keep my brother, sister and me away from that mess. Our neighborhood public school education was crap. My parents and I worked hard to find the right school and to really work hard to get there. We always had to figure out a way to do better, find the resources to make ourselves better. We knew where all the pitfalls were, we knew where all the bad was going on, and there was a sense of responsibility of going back and saying, "You've got to go and fix it. You know there're gangs in this area, you know there are bad things, there's corruption in this area. You're educated now, you're from the neighborhood, why don't you give back? Why don't you work for the government, why don't you work for a non-profit organization to really be able to give back to the community and put a stop to all the things that you had to go through?"

My dad came from Mexico City and my mom came from the border towns in Texas. There was this expectation that I would be loyal to the Chicago neighborhood I lived in, because that was my roots, that in some way I would not try to escape and be something more.

Once I got to high school, my parents just knew the best way to support me was to tell me to stay in school and do well, but there was only so much guidance they could give me. My parents went to high school and that's as far as they got. Once I got into college there was really not too much advice they could give other than just, "Hey, do well." As long as we were doing well and we were doing what we wanted to do and we didn't end up in drugs or in gangs, my parents felt that they were doing the right thing.

They did not have the expectation as some others that I grew up with that I needed to stay in my neighborhood and pursue my career within the confines of my immediate community. My parents were ecstatic when I went into Corporate America. They were very much supportive because they knew that it was going to be a steady job. They knew that I was being recognized for the work that I was doing and they saw the things that I was able to do, the opportunities that I took in different positions, the places I've gone to travel around the world and do business with, and just the things I was able to do with the income that I got. I was able to get my own place, was able to get married. I was able to buy a home, my car, and help my parents with their finances. The success came from being able to stand on my own two feet and be able to really help the family as well. I was not selling out, I was upgrading my life and future.

Being Latino means that your biggest critics are your family and your peers. We're very tough on each other. Sometimes it's competitive, sometimes it's just good banter. There's always a sense of as soon as you leave the community and you decide to go live somewhere else, you're going to do something else, it's "You sold out." They expect you to stay within the community and help it out. What happens *is, I believe, you don't always have to stay within the community, you go where the opportunity is at. You continue to take the values that you gain out of that community and bring it to another community.*

I think the other part, too, is that because you're not working for nonprofit organizations or you're not working for a government organization, it's still fine. What is your day job at a Fortune 500 company allowing you to do? Can you still be active in your community? Can you still be a part of different things? What I've seen is that it's different. I think I'm able to do more philanthropy work, community-based, working with my company rather than if I was working with a government association, because part of it, that's their job, that's their day job, it's no longer a good thing to do. They're getting paid to do that.

I'm working 10 hours a day and then maybe I might go to a meeting to kind of help with something within the Latino community and help them with a benefit. I'm giving money. I'm helping my corporation to donate money to that organization or that community program too. It's just a different feeling – a different vibe. While people are telling you, "you sold out," I think it's an opportunity to come back and say you're really not. You're really putting double effort into good causes and into your community. You are able to prepare yourself and put yourself in a position where you are better equipped to really give back.

BE INCLUSIVE

I have had co-workers look at me and say, "Okay, you got in here because of affirmative action or maybe you got in here because you actually kind of know what you're talking about."

I have worked hard to be where I am and so my response is, "I've been here for ten years and I've gotten promoted a couple of times, I'm pretty sure somebody thinks I'm doing something right." What has helped is continuing to create that path. Continuing to work in the unknown, find the right people to help you understand what's going on, because I didn't grow up with anybody who was an engineer or anybody who was on the strategy side. There was no way anybody in my neighborhood could have given me access to that. There is no way anybody in the schools that I first went to could have given me access to that. Maybe the closest I would have ever come to that was maybe a community activist or community organizer.

To be better I had to find the right people to set me on the path. I had to network with the people with the knowledge, experience and the willingness to help me. I have also had to deal with ignorant people, those who never understood how berating their words were or the impact that their negativity caused, almost pushing me to quit or just learning how to endure the pain. Eventually, you have to shake it off and just work that much harder to really show them what you're capable of accomplishing.

I've used the negative comments as fuel to understand what I never want to be in the future. If I was a mentor and I was talking to my mentee, I would want to be able to tell them, "Here are some great examples of what you do when somebody tells you that you are here because of a quota. Here's what you do when some says that affluent white guys no longer get any breaks."

For work, I have had the opportunity to travel to various countries across every continent for the exception of Antarctica. When I was asked to travel to Spain, I had to oversee the production of one of our petroleum refineries, and the moment I set foot at the facility, I was speaking Spanish with colleagues I have never met. Success in Corporate America is a balance of embracing your strengths and building allies. I use the example of my travel to Spain because I want to show you how I played up to my boss that I was such a strong asset to his team that the moment I got to the plant, I had already gained the trust of our local colleagues and began discussing the perceived problems they were having at the facility. Because my boss saw me in action, and he witnessed how comfortable I was doing business and representing his team well, he recognized my capabilities and noted to his superiors how much easier I made his job. My boss and the people I work with now say, "We kind of need you because you understand this better than we do." They include me because of my heritage and what I bring to the table.

Forge the Path for Latinos
I see myself as an employee of BP who happens to be Latino. I don't feel like I am selling out, rather I am paving a path not only for me, but those that come after me. When you want to create a path of what you want your career to look like, the first thing I would say is, "Everybody tells you to dream big and to do big things," but my advice is to do something different. Do something you have no idea about, because you may not know that you may be really good at and this is something you've been wanting to do and you just never knew it. For us who live in communities that don't have access to certain things, if you don't know it, the only way you're going to know it is when you start to put yourself out there, dip your toe in the water and seek out new experiences.

The Growth of the Latino Leader
You see a lot of the Latino finance professionals and they're doing great things and they do very well for themselves in their career, but they haven't gotten to the point where they are really making some of the big changes. When we make some of the big changes is when we become our own entrepreneurs. We're not hearing enough of a voice at these executive level management positions in Fortune 500 companies where you can really start to get the mentors that we're looking for and even just the exposure in the trenches with some of these folks who really understand how they do what they do. How do I get to be in that circle where I'm making decisions and I'm really changing a lot of, or even running a lot of these different initiatives that happen in Fortune 500 companies. It is at the C-suite level where we need to aspire to be, and provide roadmaps for others to achieve the same. Having mentors at these levels will provide the opportunities to have conversation that revolve around, "Here's what you need to do to increase your exposure or here's what your path should look like if you're thinking about getting into that area."

As Latinos we need to start leveling the playing field. We need to stop thinking that someone else will guide our career. We need to assume more personal accountability for our own professional development and apply to higher-ranking jobs, even if those jobs are at a competing company.

School Recognition

Getting a degree from just any college is not strategic enough for Corporate America. For example, typically at BP, they hire people from different schools and they groom them into rotational programs. Typically, we'll take people from Michigan State, Texas A&M, or Louisiana Tech, and they take engineers and they'll take business folks from those areas and say, "We want to hire you, we'll put you in a rotational program and we'll groom you into management positions." They do very well.

When I was in high school, I never knew those programs existed. Never had access to that, so I was kind of late to the game. I kind of had to fight a little bit harder to say, "Okay, I didn't come from those schools, I didn't come from an engineering school. I went to a local school, my background is not engineering, but I did I graduate with a Business degree." Now I have to prove my worth.

The other part that was even tougher was that my background was different. I maybe had one or two internships that I could use as experience, but most of my professional experience was working blue-collar jobs. I was either working at my father's plant where he was a plant manager, and I was working on the line or I was working on maintenance and I was working on stuff to earn some money to pay for tuition. I also worked in restaurants too. I didn't have access to those corporate internships, so I was not able to compete solely on my professional experience because I truly did not have any professional experience. So instead, I competed on my ability to be a resourceful go-getter and a leader. That's all I had and that's what I played up during my interviews. Obviously it worked, but it did not come without multiple rounds of interviews with various division leaders to assess if I was telling the truth.

Accepting a Corporation Relocation Offer

My family is in Chicago, and family is extremely important to me. They have not left because Chicago is home – but in the corporate world this family attachment and value can be considered a hindrance. Corporate America expects employees to move for their jobs, and to move often. I have made a personal decision to not accept corporate relocation offers. I think I have missed opportunities.

If I had known that this was the career path to take, to be more competitive, I think it would have given me a significant advantage if I had been mobile. I don't think it holds me back as it used to, because I finally feel like I got to a point where I'm at the big kids' table and I'm able to compete, which gives me leverage and more choices. I earned my seat, now I start talking about how do I get to the executive table. How do we really start doing that? However, if I had moved earlier in my career, perhaps I would have gotten to this point faster. It's hard to tell, but moving around for the company does help you move up the corporate ladder.

If I were to give someone tangible advice on how to pursue their career to achieve success in Corporate America, this is the roadmap that I would offer for them to consider:

1) *You will reinvent yourself multiple times throughout your career. Try new things and don't be afraid to change if something does not work out.*
2) *Aim high, apply to work for some of the best companies that you think you will do well. Get that name recognition on your resume because it will help distinguish your personal brand.*
3) *Accept every challenge that is offered to you. While I did not relocate for the company and I had my personal reasons, I could have made it work.*
4) *Believe in the mantra, "Success through Yes!" Consider relocation opportunities*
5) *Find a mentor, find a champion, find an executive who will advocate for you when you are being evaluated behind closed doors*
6) *Pursue a master's degree from a top school because it just helps.*
7) *Be prepared to answer the question, "What do you want to do with your career?" It will require you to do some soul searching, but will show them that you have ambition and you possess a plan on how to get there.*
8) *Be results oriented. Your office will be filled with people who say why things cannot be done, but be that voice that says why it can be done.*
9) *Get involved in committees or tasks force. Success in Corporate America is not solely measured by how well you do your job, because you are expected*

to do that well. Success is measured by how much of a leader you are when asked to do things outside of your job description.

10) *Finally, understand that you got hired because you are expected to possess the hard skills. The advancement happens when you demonstrate you have the soft skills. Can you manage people, do you present well, are you willing take a risk and be held accountable for the result. Be confident in your abilities.*

CHAPTER 6

The Future of Latinos

• • •

OFTEN TIMES, I REFLECT ON how much our community has accomplished. We are living in a generation where a significant percentage of our own people are doing well. While we still have struggles, our role models are growing. Our influence is growing and the number of people who look like us on the national stage and serve as inspirations, whether it be in politics, law, business or civil rights is also growing. And as the United States Census has forecast, our presence is this country will continue to grow.

I think of my parents, how they were brave enough to envision a life in America, even though they did not have a roadmap on how to live life in America. They just did their best to live. Today, we have more leaders that are Latino and believe in helping our community to further develop itself. We have associations dedicated to help our community with educational and career opportunities. There are employee resource groups within corporations whose intent is to help people like you become acclimated with their corporate culture so you can be a success and reach your potential. Your job is to further develop yourself. You are one of our future leaders.

Throughout this book, I shared with you multiple personal stories from Latinos who are at various stages of their lives, from recent college graduates to established business professional. Their stories illustrated what they do, how they developed a mindset to overcome their objections and how they pursued their goals. Those stories should have generated ideas for you to craft your personal roadmap to achieve the success you seek in your career. Now, success is one of those funny words because it has a subjective definition. Success can be defined by monetary compensation, title, or quality of life. Whether you aspire to be the president of a Fortune 100 corporation or just to have enough money to pay your bills and lead a happy life, the roadmap you create from the ideas generated from reading this book will provide you with a plan to get there. Your success will have a direct impact on the trajectory of our Latino community in America. Your personal influence will shape the rising generation of Latinos because they will see how you approach your career and your personal life. If they see that you are happy, then they too will want to follow in your footsteps and your influence will create a generation of motivated Latinos because they will want to be like you.

While I see the future of our Latino community to be filled with great optimism and promise, I challenge you to create your 3-year plan to achieve your goal. As one of my colleagues said to me, "A roadmap will have twist and turns. There will be a few corners that you will not see and steep climbs that you did not expect. Regardless, a roadmap will show you where your destination is and how far away you are from achieving your goal." I need you to make your plan. Get motivated. Figure out your next step, and do not create a roadmap that goes beyond three years because anything too far out becomes too hard to manage and impossible to implement.

Your career is important. While an MBA may not be required to achieve your goals, having one sure makes the path easier and quicker. If you want to grow in your company and you believe that earning an MBA will help your make a leap to catapult your career forward and salary upward, then draft your roadmap. Decide what title you want to pursue, research which business schools attract the corporations you want to work for, assess your level of competitiveness, and join like-minded people who share you vision and goals so you can support each other as you begin your journey. Give yourself an end date and tell yourself you want to start school two years from today and create the roadmap to get you there!

If you want to become a senior executive at your company, begin networking with the current senior executives. Share your ambition with the decision makers. If you are too nervous to have that conversation, find 20 seconds of courage to send an email to your boss and ask her/him for their opinion or solicit their help to socialize your ambition on your behalf. If would do not believe you can grow any further at your company, then find a way to get out and pursue your ambition somewhere that will value your skills and contributions. The power is within you. Create your action plan, develop your roadmap, and stay committed.

The difference between you and someone who tried will be that you did not lose faith in yourself. You will have challenges. You will have disappointments and you will have detractors who will place roadblocks in front of you, but once again, that's okay. It's okay because no one will care if you have folks against you. That is not their problem, it will be yours to overcome and it will be sweet when you do. Focus on your gifts, talents, and ambition.

You are Latino! You were born to excel regardless of the challenges you have and will encounter. And just like our people who came before you, you too will **RISE UP, AND SEGUIR ADELANTE!**

About the Author

• • •

OVER THE PAST 15 YEARS, Jesse has developed a rich career in corporate strategy, business development and risk management, working for Fortune 100 companies such as Dun & Bradstreet, General Motors and most recently as Corporate Strategy Officer for the Volkswagen Group of America's financing subsidiary, VW Credit, Inc. Jesse is an award-winning speaker, ranked as one of Toastmasters International's top humorist speakers and is a member of the National Speakers Association. Passionate about personal economic empowerment, he provides a roadmap for young professionals to succeed in their careers by delivering multi-cultural, comprehensive, and innovative programs that address social, academic, and professional needs.

Jesse has been quoted by the Wall Street Journal, USA Today, and has been a featured guest on National Public Radio (NPR) Talk of the Nation for their "The Art and Science of Motivation" segment. He is recognized for delivering dynamic presentations that are motivational, inspirational, and humorous.

As an alumnus of Syracuse University (B.S. Communications) and Georgetown University (MBA), Jesse is proud to call himself an Orange-Hoya. Jesse considers Washington D.C. home and volunteers his time with the local chapter of the Cystic Fibrosis Foundation and as an alumni interviewer for his alma mater, Phillips Exeter Academy.

www.ingramcontent.com/pod-product-compliance
Lightning Source LLC
Chambersburg PA
CBHW070908160426
43193CB00011B/1408